Jesus Loves You . . .
This I Know

Jesus L♥ves You this I know

craig gross
and
jason harper

BakerBooks

a division of Baker Publishing Group
Grand Rapids, Michigan

Published by Baker Books
a division of Baker Publishing Group
P.O. Box 6287, Grand Rapids, MI 49516-6287
www.bakerbooks.com

Printed in the United States of America

Library of Congress Cataloging-in-Publication Data
Gross, Craig, 1975–
    Jesus loves you—this I know / Craig Gross and Jason Harper.
        p.   cm.
    ISBN 978-0-8010-1329-4 (cloth)
    1. God—Love. 2. Jesus Christ—Person and offices. I. Harper, Jason, 1971–
II. Title.
BT140.G76 2009
231.6—dc22   2009013759

ISBN 978-0-8010-7252-9 (ITPE)

Craig Gross is represented by The Nashville Agency, P.O. Box 110909, Nashville, TN 37222. www.nashvilleagency.com.

The authors would like to acknowledge Drew Melton, who created the original art for the front cover, and Adam Palmer, who provided the first edit of the manuscript.

To protect the privacy of those whose stories are shared by the authors, some details and names have been changed.

Interior design by Sarah Lowrey Brammeier

Jesu
Lo

Contents

Acknowledgments

We are overwhelmed by the truth that was lived out in the life of Jesus. Those traits are lived out every day in our wives. Jeanette and Lynette make each of us better. They are strong and focused, compassionate and consistent. They both put up with the controlled chaos that comes with being married to us. Love is not a strong enough word for our thankfulness.

So many people have helped reinforce the scripture's value in our life. To them, we acknowledge and dedicate our efforts of this work.

Ron Jeremy. We love you for who you are and recognize the road to transformation is long and rough. Keep walking with us. Our commitment to you is unconditional. Thank you for listening, debating, and ultimately respecting the message of Christ.

Gay Joe. Your vulnerability and complete compassion toward humanity have taught us so much. Thank you for trusting us. In the middle of cultural turmoil, we hope our conversations scribed on these pages will increase the civility and empathy.

For those who surround us each day. Your willingness to run with us makes the journey worth it. The best is yet to come.

Lastly, we would like to thank our pastors who have spoken into our lives over the last few years—Rob Bell, Bryan Johnston, and Rick Cole. Your support, confidence, and courage to lead have modeled for both of us what we want to be.

Introduction

The message of Jesus is as simple and concise as the song many of us learned and sang in preschool: *Jesus loves me, this I know.*

Me.

You.

Practically everyone knows that little ditty.

But many don't know its truth and power. The first two words do not inspire a lot of emotion. "Jesus loves." It is when one gets to the "me," the "you," that things get more complicated.

Jesus Loves **You**.

The all-encompassing "you" means that the love of Jesus leaves no one out. We hope this book will compel people to see that, regardless of where they have been or what they have gone through, there is a love that endures all things.

If you're forgotten . . . love finds.

If you're broken . . . love mends.

If you're an outcast . . . love includes.

No matter what . . . believe us, love works.

Whether you see Jesus as a teacher or a rabbi, a revolutionary or a savior, one thing is certain: he had a powerful effect on people.

If you have been a Christian for a while, we want to help you review the footsteps of Jesus. We're trying to rethink his approach to a hurting humanity and strive to live it out; we hope you'll join us.

If you have never considered Jesus, we'll provide a peek into the daily interactions he had. You'll see that with Jesus, a miracle is always one breath away.

Jesus started a revolution by willfully submitting to the greatest of causes.

Love.

These pages tell the story of how Jesus loved. Why he loved. And what that means to you.

Craig

Over the course of the week, Jason and I find ourselves hanging out with people who are not the typical crowd for an ordained pastor. To most Christians, our social circles look like a tangled web of contradiction. But I have discovered that through contradiction and confusion can come greater clarity.

I am a pastor. I am married with two kids, and I have one goal: to tell others about the Jesus who changed my life so he can change theirs. It sounds cliché, but I have given my life to spiritually leading other people to a life worth living—a life where the actions, ideas, and character of Jesus are apparent. The ways of Jesus work, and I want to communicate that to anyone who will listen.

As I write this, I am thirty-three years old. I was once a youth pastor, and many of my former youth pastor peers have gone on to become senior pastors (or "lead pastors," as the current trend puts it) in churches across the country. One of these great friends is Jason Harper, another former youth pastor turned . . . well, I'll get to that.

I am known by a lot of people as the "Porn Pastor" because I started a ministry called www.XXXchurch.com seven years ago that has taken me around the world speaking out on issues of pornography while also loving those in the porn industry. We go to porn conventions and hand out Bibles that proudly proclaim "Jesus Loves Porn Stars." We drive a bus up and down the Las Vegas strip that says "Jesus Loves Sin City." So, writing a book called *Jesus Loves You* is one of my biggest thrills, because I have witnessed firsthand the healing power of this message. Those words, no matter how they are stated, should not be misunderstood.

Jesus loves . . . now, fill in the blank. Think of crooks and soccer moms, prostitutes and pastors, porn stars and CEOs. Jesus loves every one of them. To Jesus, we're all just people who need God to save us from the mess we are in and lead us to a better way.

Back to Jason. He is technically a pastor, but I call him the Cable Guy. Somebody told him he had it too easy when it came to talking to people about Jesus because he worked in a church. Jason took that as a challenge and accepted a job in one of the most dreaded trades: bill collections for a television cable company.

He figured that if God can work there, God can work anywhere.

Believing the Bible is true and the principles of Jesus are transferable to any venue, Jason, our resident Cable Guy, wanted to answer these questions:

Could an ordinary pastor practice what he preached?

Could the methods of reaching people taught in the church on Sunday hold water with the Cable Guy collecting outstanding payments on Monday?

As an outreach pastor, Jason Harper stepped beyond the pulpit of his local church and into the homes of his local neighborhood to experience real stories of real people transformed by a real Savior.

So, as you read this book, don't assume that because two pastors wrote it, we are your typical Sunday morning TV preachers. We aren't. We spend most of our time outside the church with unchurched people. We don't care if they are people who can't pay their cable bill or people who perform for videos that show up on late-night cable.

Doesn't matter what you do or who you are: Jesus. Loves. You.

The Problem

Over the last two thousand years, Jesus' vision and values have been distorted, twisted, hijacked, tweaked, relabeled, and distorted again. Those who have followed Jesus have subtly, over time, redefined his plan to fit their particular motives, their agendas . . . their worlds. Now the concept of living a sacrificial life that is attractive *to* the broken has largely been replaced with a religious exclusivity that has *made* people broken.

> **Doesn't matter what you do or who you are: Jesus. Loves. You.**

In the hands of everyone from derailed evangelicals to deceptive evangelists, Jesus' message has been hijacked.

Take a look back over time. From day to day, to months and years and decades and centuries, the plotline has remained the same. The Savior of the world has been sabotaged.

It may have started as small and subtle—and probably not that harmful, actually. Perhaps a quote taken out of context here, a little misunderstanding there. But eventually these little distortions, these little twistings, turned into all-out manipulations and misrepresentations of the King of the universe.

The most effective hijacking of Jesus and his will has come from those who claim to live for him but really don't. Shortly after the first millennium ended, in AD 1095, Gode-froy de Bouillon, a French knight, led the First Crusade and founded the Kingdom of Jerusalem. Religion was leveraged and legislated. Essentially, if a person didn't believe in the established order, they were ostracized, isolated from the mainstream—sometimes even killed. Later, the infamous Constantine used the name of Jesus to manipulate, murder, and monopolize.[1]

Let me give just one example. Constantine controlled commerce. When shippers would try to sell or buy, there were two menus: one for Christians and one for non-Christians. If someone was trying to save a buck, they simply lied and claimed to be Christian, even though they had no allegiance to Jesus, no relationship with him. This form of exclusive commerce killed the distinctive identity of Christians and made Jesus into a coupon.

Fast-forward a few centuries to the Crusades. Christians were at war with Muslims. Christians rolled into villages and inquired of the leadership, "Who is of Christ?" Those who would not confess Christ were promptly beheaded. It was an early form of terrorism!

Over time in these regions, selfish ambition and the pursuit of political power was cloaked in Christ's name. Resentment boiled against anyone who believed. The chasm between believers and unbelievers increased. People used religion to steal and extort. Jesus, it came to be understood, was not about giving, only getting.

His message, sacrifice, and even his name were hijacked.

Yet there have always been the faithful. Think about all the hospitals, schools, and charities followers of Jesus have built. Think about all the kids who are fed and housed in the developing world because of Christians.

Christianity is a mixed bag.

Recently, a car pulled out in front of me. Its bumper was plastered with stickers. One said, "Follow me to my Baptist church!" while another said, "Nuke Iran."

Hijacked.

Inch by inch, from his thorn-scarred head to his nail-holed feet, Jesus has been resketched until the picture no longer matches the man. In the church, one pew is filled with revolutionaries who want to love and lead people, while another pew seats people who aren't even aware they're in it for themselves.

Many people I talk to see Jesus as somebody who micromanages the events of day-to-day living. They think Jesus' only desire is to take away freedoms and fun and to exclude every person who doesn't always say and do the right things. The real Jesus had nothing to do with that kind of program.

He came to free people from slavery to the law and to be the bridge between God and humanity.

Our world is in the midst of global chaos, and we desperately need a Savior. As I write this, over fifty-nine countries are engaged in some level of war.[2] According to the SIPRI (Stockholm International Peace Research Institute) and population data, "about 2.15 billion people—a third of the world's population—live in countries currently beset by armed conflict."[3] Extreme poverty affects a third of the world's population. Nearly a billion people do not have access to clean water. Over one million people have lost their jobs in the US in the first part of 2009. If the world was ever primed to hear, accept, and walk with Jesus, it is now.

> **The real Jesus had nothing to do with that kind of program. He came to free people from slavery to the law and to be the bridge between God and humanity.**

The chasm between those who live like Jesus and those who are still asking what he would do is increasing. And a third group does not know what or who to believe.

A Conversation

Recently Jason and I were in Nashville. I was doing a talk on the degenerating effects of porn. Across the stage was Ron Jeremy, one of the most popular porn stars in America. Ron and I often speak on college campuses to explain our different views, and over the course of these discussions, we have gotten to know each other quite well. Watching the presentation backstage were Jason and two other friends, Greg and John, who arrange these college speaking engagements for Ron and me.

After the presentation, Ron vanished to his room, and Jason and I went out to eat with Greg and John. From snippets of past conversations with Greg and from hearing about some of his rants, it was clear to me that God was nowhere on his radar. But he liked talking with me, he said, because he saw something different in me.

Maybe tonight was different. Maybe it had nothing to do with God. Maybe he was probing deeper because I had embraced Ron as a friend and not judged him.

Before the main dish hit the table, Greg leaned toward me and spoke with an inquisitive tone that made me feel like he was really digging for some answers. "Craig, your belief is very different from what I have seen. The Christians I've met are jerks."

I knew this was a broad generalization from Greg. Part of me agreed with him.

Before I could respond, Greg continued.

"Can I ask you a question?"

"Sure," I said, hoping it would be about the presentation or, even better, what I wanted for dinner. No chance.

"Who is God? Who wrote the Bible and how do we know that it is real?"

I paused for a moment and swallowed the rest of my fried pickle. Then, in my most clear and concise fashion, I started with the first question and moved on through. I knew Greg wasn't baiting me—this was a genuine quest in his heart, and I wanted to be clear. I asked Jason for his input.

Together we walked through each element that makes the Bible different from any other document. We talked about the Dead Sea Scrolls, the fulfilled prophecies of Isaiah, and the historical evidence from the writings of Josephus.

Over the course of thirty minutes, our conversation hit on the historical, mathematical, even the scientific value and authenticity of scripture.

Then it ramped up. Greg kept digging. His persistence was genuine. In no way did I feel like he wanted to debate me; instead, I felt like he wanted to dig through all his preconceived notions—notions planted by Christians who peddled an imitation Jesus.

As these thoughts dawned on me, I could feel myself getting angry and sidetracked. Not at the conversation, but at Christians who had done so much damage.

Greg's words snapped me back into focus.

"Why do you claim there is only one way to God . . . this Jesus story?"

I pondered, looked at Jason, took a deep breath, then spoke. "All of our futures really hang on that answer!"

We honed in on the defining factors of Jesus, and I could tell Jason wanted to get into what had become a two-way conversation.

"Jason, you wanna jump in here?"

Jason began to scratch out the difference between Jesus and other world religious leaders. I talked about the difference between the Jesus of scripture and the Jesus whom Greg and John had seen sold on TV.

Those two pictures were worlds apart.

As we wrapped up the three-hour dinner, the restaurant was nearly empty. And so was my heart. I had this empty place that had been dug up by the realization that Greg and John had never been given a clear explanation of the Jesus I live for.

They spoke of the many times Christians had told them they were going to hell. They spoke of moments they thought were spiritual, but never could attach that feeling to Jesus. They spoke of a hunger to go deeper, but had never been invited into a conversation that would allow them to belong.

Re-Branding Jesus

I realized in that moment this is where the re-branding of Jesus needs to occur. Western culture has set up a progress-based system for advancing toward God.

Let me explain. For a long time Christians have been taught a three-step approach to God. It starts with belief. Essentially, if you believe the right things, it will lead to a change in behavior. When you have changed your behavior, you will be accepted by the church. Believe, Behave, Belong.

If you believe this way, you will behave this way, and if you behave this way, you can belong here. This is preached, modeled, and affirmed in thousands of churches across America.

It's time to flip this. The Jesus of scripture reached out and loved people regardless of where they were. It is essential to show people that they can belong in your world even if they don't act, think, behave, or believe like you.

Imagine a church or community where Jesus was communicated in such a way that everyone belonged. They were included. And from this feeling of belonging, over time the message of Jesus made an impact on their belief. And from that newfound fullness of God, their behavior changed.

If this practice won out over religious dogma, rooted in rules and regulations, more people would find hope in the authentic Christ.

That's what Greg and John needed. That's what Greg and John wanted.

We parted ways for the evening, and Jason was quiet the rest of the night. I was too.

Before we all went our ways, I got to tie up some loose ends with John and Greg. Both thanked me for the dinner and dialogue. The next morning I received an email from Greg. I won't forget his words: "Craig, the time you and Jason spent with us last night was awesome. I told my girlfriend that if I met more Christians like you guys, maybe my beliefs would be different."

> **It is essential to show people that they can belong in your world even if they don't act, think, behave, or believe like you.**

I don't tell this story to pat myself on the back. Not even close. It's meant to bring perspective to the discussion.

Greg and John had been sold a fabricated counterfeit picture of Jesus. Sure it looked the part, but under examination, the value was not there. They had only seen a plastic version of a priceless Christ.

For too long he has been misquoted and misrepresented by misguided, if well-meaning, people.

The bottom line is this: as the chasm between the real Jesus and the counterfeit Jesus gets wider, Jesus becomes more and more irrelevant.

That's why we wrote this book. It is about two guys who love Jesus and believe Jesus loves you just as much as he loves us. It is about rebuilding, restating, and reinstituting the hope and faith that was birthed at the cross where Jesus died.

This book is about two guys who love Jesus and believe Jesus loves you just as much as he loves us.

The results are in. Those outside of the church with limited or no faith are jaded, feeling bitter and betrayed. Those within faith circles who look down on them are judgmental.

The jaded and the judgmental. Both need to be reconnected to a simple truth: Jesus loves them. Regardless of how they got to this place, both are disconnected from the full purpose they were created to complete.

This we know.

1. Bruno Bleckmann, "Sources for the History of Constantine," *Cambridge Companion to the Age of Constantine*, ed. Noel Lenski (Cambridge: Cambridge University Press, 2006). Cambridge Collections Online, Cambridge University Press. Accessed 6 March 2009.

2. http://www.peace2k.org/atwar.html.

3. http://answers.google.com/answers/threadview/id/405897.html.

Jesu

L

Jason

Her voice hurt my ears. Literally. Over time her words sounded like an echo of the high-pitched, frenzied static of Charlie Brown's annoying teacher . . . *Wah wha, wah, wah wha whine*.

She probably didn't mean it to be so cutting. Yet with every breath she took, I had to take a deeper one. She stood across the book table where I was promoting the writing project Craig and I had just completed, *The Gutter*. She was a nice-looking lady, but I must admit I was tired of looking at her.

Her words hurt, but I could not deny the truth of what she was saying. I had just finished a talk, encouraging Christians to move from the ordinary monotony of belief to the highways and byways of boldness. An essential message: get in the gutter and share Jesus with love and kindness to every person. Without an agenda, communicate the story of your connection to Jesus and allow it to impact the disconnected.

At the end of the talk, I gave a simple, three-step process that was a low-risk/high-return method of biblical outreach. I'd taken these steps from an assortment of illustrations from

Jesus' life and teaching models from great churches. Nothing profound, just doable stuff. It was a simple message that communicated Jesus' love for the disconnected.

Having finished my talk, I sat down to answer some questions. And that's when this woman nailed me.

Clutching her large black-leather Bible, she blasted away. "You work in a church," she said. "You don't know what it's like to be in a secular workplace, dealing with cranky customers all day. You try to shine a light there!"

At least that was the gist of what she said. It just took her a few minutes to get it all out.

I listened, taking it all in. I realized as she talked that my whole existence as an outreach pastor was inward.

Ingrown.

Sunday I was at the church. Monday through Thursday . . . church. From morning until evening . . . church. On the rare occasion of a free Saturday, I stayed secluded in my Christian circle or my immediate family.

This woman used my employment at a church as a rope to hang me. Maybe I really *didn't* understand her struggles to survive in the secular world. What was it like to have a jerk for a boss or office peers who spoke debauchery all day? Had I forgotten what it was like to live amongst those who didn't look like me, act like me, talk like me, or believe what I believed? I became frustrated.

Who was I to be delivering a message on outreach? If asked, those around me on a daily basis would have said I was always with the unchurched—at least compared to others who are in the vocational church. Maybe that is what has been the downfall within the church.

Maybe church leadership across America, as with me, had gotten so busy doing "the ministry" that we forgot the main point of ministry.

These reflections quickly faded when I realized Miss Whiney was still complaining. Finally, I spoke to her in short, but kind words.

"Lady, you're right," I said. "I need to find people who are doing this and then tell their story. But the methods of Jesus worked."

I mentally stumbled away. Though I didn't have an answer to combat the secular workplace, I did understand his life. Still, it didn't soothe the futility and frustration that came with working in a church. Over time I had been inoculated from the very world I was told to love and lead with compassion and kindness.

And yet I knew one thing: God would never ask me or anyone else to be a light and then not equip us to do it. My dilemma was to figure out how to do it in the *secular* workforce, when my current workforce was exclusively in the church.

I had to find the answer.

> **Over time I had been inoculated from the very world I was told to love and lead with compassion and kindness.**

The Grand Experiment

I started thinking about how Jesus interacted with the world around him. Jesus mastered the critics. Usually he answered their challenges with a question. When the Pharisees were testing him with questions meant to trap him, Jesus responded with his own questions, one after the other, until they could no longer reply. His questions were answers.

Asking questions connects people to a conversation. Jesus was about connecting to the disconnected.

Every step of the way, Jesus communicated two simple messages, depending on who was listening: grace and law. To the religious who were cynical and judgmental, he offered the Law. On the other side were people without religious convictions. They were not part of the religious movement. They were common people with common needs. Jesus loved them with authentic compassion and practical help. In their broken and lost state, he offered grace that came in the promise of wholeness.

Whenever he prepared to reach out to them, he started by meeting a practical need. He offered food to the hungry and then followed it up by saying he was the Bread of Life. He healed blind eyes and then invited people to use their restored eyesight to see the Truth.

Remember the Bible story about the religious leaders catching a woman in the act of adultery?[1] Dragged by her hair, this outcast of society stood naked before Jesus. Her accusers wanted her head; she just wanted out. Jesus protected her by asking her accusers to throw stones if their closets were without skeletons. And they left.

As she stood there, he simply said, "Go and sin no more." Jesus connected with her in spite of her sin. Though she was disconnected, he connected.

It was the perfect picture of two worlds coming together: the practical, the spiritual. The earthly intertwined with the heavenly.

Profound. Purposeful. Promising.

Jesus' example was clear. Meet people where they are. Look for an opportunity to love someone by meeting a practical need. Then wait for the spiritual doors to open.

Jesus' method in this scenario stirred me. Why was he so committed to love? Perhaps it was because he knew every hurt that was experienced in every heart. He knew every circumstance that caused people to become disconnected. He loved them all: the outcast, the downtrodden, the reclusive and alone.

As I started driving home, I wanted answers, but the questions kept coming—

What could I do?

What would I do?

How did I get so spiritually secluded?

Where did I go wrong?

How did I get so removed from the very group Jesus implored me to reach?

How did my circle of influence become ingrown?

I needed more. I needed a rediscovery of the reason I believed.

By the time I got home, I couldn't wait to read through the Gospels (the first four books of the New Testament) to study what Jesus did to connect to the hurting and helpless.

The lady's words kept running through my head: "But how can you tell me how to love in the workplace when your workplace is a church? You ought to spend a day in my job."

They echoed in my ears like an annoying drip from a rusty faucet. I searched my mind for a solution as I devoured stories about Jesus.

The Cable Guy

I wanted a belief laboratory—a way to test whether Jesus' methods still worked today. But if I was going to do this, I wanted to do it big. Not a simple, one-day excursion to share Jesus in the inner city. I'd already done that. Many times. I needed to find a way to surround myself with those who didn't believe like me, didn't respect me, didn't know me, didn't want to hear from me.

I'll get a second job, I thought. I could get a part-time gig, a couple days a week maybe. My wife worked at the local country club; maybe I could pick up a few hours there. The problem with that was, everyone there knew I was Lynette's husband, a pastor. If I went that route, the project lost its authenticity before it started.

> **I wanted a belief laboratory—a way to test whether Jesus' methods still worked today.**

What if I submerged myself in a job everyone hates? *What's the most hated job in the world?* I wondered. What if I could find a job where I would initially be hated and despised?

What if I spent a year in a job whose very name provoked disgust?

It needed to be a legal job, so "dope dealer" wouldn't work.

I asked my wife, "What do you think is the most hated job in the world?" She paused. I could see the wheels turning. I was thinking maybe a prison guard. Or a policeman. I got it . . . a politician! Yet with each profession I could think of, a reason surfaced for why it could not be the most hated.

Finally, I landed on one that fit the bill. Collectors are hated, mostly because their only job is to take. Take money. Security. Peace of mind.

Even if you're current on your payments, the mere thought of having to be around a collections agent disgusts most people. I wanted to create an experiment where I could operate under the cloak of the hated. I wanted to see if, while collecting delinquent payments, I could still connect with people.

I took a one-day-a-week collections job working for a national cable company. They trained me and sent me out. If I couldn't collect and the customer was more than ninety days past due, I was supposed to disconnect their service.

People hated me, all right. Imagine walking into a home and disconnecting Oprah or ESPN. As I went about my work, I was full-on accosted, threatened, chased by dogs, and offered dope to ignore the work order.

People around me wondered, "Why would an outreach pastor step from behind the pulpit on Sunday into the cut-throat community of collections on Monday?"

I wish I had the space to describe the interactions I had over that year. For fifty-two weeks I traveled to more than thirty homes a week. Sometimes they owed a ton, sometimes only a few bucks. Regardless of the amount, I learned a lot about human dignity, isolation, and broken families. I had a host of encounters with people who were so disconnected from life and their destiny that they virtually gave up.

Why was Jesus so committed to love? Perhaps it was because, as God, he knew everything. He knew every hurt that was experienced in every heart. He knew every circumstance that caused people to cut off interaction and become isolationists. He loved the disconnected. He searched for them: the outcast, the downtrodden, the recluse.

Willie the Wino

One morning in mid-March when it was unseasonably cold, I began my collections work questioning my commitment to keep this experiment going for a whole year. The early morning air burned my nose with each breath as I got into my truck.

I drove on the backroads to an address in the high foothills of Northern California, where a guy named Willie was ninety-two days delinquent for over $120. Rarely did someone settle up when the bill was that large. Usually the customer let me cut the cable and then a month or two later had it turned back on using a wife's or kid's name on the account.

As the road narrowed, I noticed that the drizzle streaking the windshield had now turned to a light snow. The farther I climbed in elevation, the thicker the snow became. With only a brief pause to lock in my Toyota's four-wheel drive, I arrived at a scarce development of small, one-acre lots lined with ranch homes built in the late 1960s. This part of the foothills had become home to many former Bay Area and Sacramento residents who wanted to leave the rat race but couldn't give up their jobs. Many settled for living over ninety minutes out of town.

Peering through a fogged window and using wipers worn from heavy winter use, I managed to find Willie's address. The freakish snowstorm had covered his sidewalk and driveway, leaving a layer of six or more inches of fresh powder on his small house. Knocking on the door, ready to pitch my Cable Guy introduction, I saw that the house was dead silent. It looked abandoned. While smoke billowed from the smokestacks of neighboring homes, Willie's house looked and felt cold. I peeked through the side door window; all the lights were off. No sign of life anywhere. Stacks of paper everywhere. Dirty dishes. Clothes thrown all over the place.

A ray of sun broke through the clouds and lit the east side of the house. Again I knocked on the door while looking for movement of any kind. Slowly, beneath a pile of clothes, a grey-haired man with an unshaven face started to stir. This guy's in trouble, I thought, as he thrashed and fumbled around. He needed help. My heart raced, and I started pounding on a window. He looked at me, confused. My collections job had turned into a human rescue mission.

I was unsure what this guy would be like when he opened the door. Angry? Crazy?

The door slowly cracked open. Standing before me was an emaciated grandpa whose eyes dripped with desperation.

Hurting from the cold, hungry from empty cupboards, Willie was scared. Warmed only by whiskey, he stood thin and emaciated. After his paranoid panning back and forth over my shoulder, he finally invited

My collections job had turned into a human rescue mission.

me in. Within seconds of stepping inside, the decay and mold of rotting food and backed-up sinks plagued the air. The home felt dark. His soul felt darker.

I explained I was the Cable Guy. I felt guilty. This man had nothing, and I was going to cut the cable. It was irrelevant. TVs don't work without electricity, and I doubted Willie had electricity. When I asked, he looked puzzled.

"Do I have electricity? What kind of question is that? Of course I do. I would die without it." Willie was feisty. He stepped over empty bottles of whiskey, piles of cat feces, empty ravioli cans, and boxes of empty crackers to flip the light switch. A dim ceiling light flickered, and Willie began to tell me the story of how he had been disconnected from society for the last few years. Willie was a loner, an alcoholic. He needed to know the love of Jesus.

After talking to him for two hours, I stood to leave. I was a third of the way through my once-a-week workday and had not completed a single house. But I had listened to a hurting old man who had experienced more pain in the past several years than I had experienced my entire life. He had lost his wife, his mother, and a friend to cancer. His house had been robbed. He had been the victim of a thieving and meth-using neighbor who wrote checks to herself out of his account, the last being only the day before. In the carbon copy of Willie's check, the memo read, "Willie's Groceries." Over two hundred spent on "groceries" less than twenty-four hours prior and not a single crumb in the house. He'd been scammed. I flipped through the checkbook and saw monthly totals that were over $1000 made to her, in her handwriting.

I drove to the store and got him some basic foods that he could prepare. When I showed him the bananas, Willie started to cry. All he could muster was, "Why?"

God's love extends to the disconnected and to the least as if it were to Jesus himself. It builds a bridge that reconnects the disconnected back to humanity. Willie nibbled down a banana as I loaded into my truck to leave.

I didn't bring up the cable collections. I couldn't. This old guy had told me the best part of the day was watching reruns of Andy Griffith. I slipped out, and he never asked why I came.

That night I couldn't eat dinner. I just talked. I had to tell my family about Willie. I made mental calculations about how many days the small amount of food would last. My wife suggested I go back the next day. I did, and every week for the next six months.

After I'd seen Willie sober for three Mondays, I asked him if he had kicked the bottle. He assured me he had not but he didn't want to be "loopy" if I was stopping by. Willie was connecting to people. I started telling his story to my friends. My friends told him stories about me. We laughed.

Some friends of mine rallied and paid off his cable bill. Others helped balance his checkbook. A couple guys paid a visit to the thief next door. Their law enforcement knowledge motivated her to steer clear of Willie. They said Willie was their friend.

I felt as if I was born to be the Cable Guy. The reality is, I was born to tell people that Jesus loved them. Willie got it. Willie believed.

By mid-August I learned that Willie had a daughter in Reno. On a whim I looked in his phone book by his rotary phone and saw a number under "daughter." I called it. It was her. I had to explain to her that I had struck up a six-month friendship with her estranged alcoholic father, who lived far off the beaten path in a mountain home. I told her when I found him. I told her he had met many of my friends. I told her we had cleaned his house and got him a steady supply line of groceries.

I asked her how long it had been since they talked; she said it had been since her wedding four years before. Her voice cracked: "I have got to see him."

Less than two weeks later, Willie would be packed up and moving to Reno, reconnected.

The last time I left his place was hard. He was moving the next morning, and I didn't want to be there, so I said goodbye and hugged him. I snapped a photo or two before it was time to go. I was moved. As I backed out the driveway, he hollered for me to roll down my window.

These were the last words Willie said to me: "God sent you here."

Just six months earlier, Willie was alone, nearly frozen, with no food in his cupboards. He had no family nearby and was the victim of elder abuse. He had every intention of drinking himself to death.

These were the last words Willie said to me: "God sent you here."

But Jesus had other intentions. His love for the disconnected moved a pastor to become a cable guy, driving up snowy backroads to collect a bill. Truth be told, I never saw a dime from Willie, but I would give up all the riches in the world for what I did receive.

---

1. See John 8:1–11.

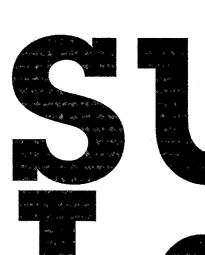

Jesu
Lo

ls

ves

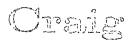

Craig

This world is full of broken people. I have seen my share of brokenness, but of all I've seen, I still have never heard a story that made more sense of Jesus' love for the broken than that of my wife, Jeanette. I'll let her tell it to you . . .

In January 1993, I was having the time of my life. I only had one semester of high school left, I was starting a new relationship with a great guy, and I had finally found some very close friends.

One girl, Shannon, was someone who, no matter what kind of day I was having, would always make my world brighter. We had spent hours having in-depth conversations about life, relationships, family, and our dreams for the future. She was the girl in school who was everyone's friend. She was not shy about talking to anyone, even if it meant talking to the "uncool" or "unpopular." She had such a positive outlook on everything and was a good and loyal friend. Finally, I had found someone who understood me and who inspired me to be a better person.

I had found a true best friend.

The summer before our senior year started, we spent a lot of time together. We had such a blast going to the beach and cruising around in my VW Jetta. She was a positive influence on me, unlike friends in the past who were always out to get me into trouble. We hung out often with another girl, Nikki, and we became our own little group, always together.

One day after school, Nikki and Shannon were headed back to Nikki's house to drop off her brother and his two friends at their house. They were planning to go to the gym after that, but they never made it to their first stop.

The police don't know what happened for sure. What they do know is that as Nikki was driving her '80s Honda Civic, she swerved into oncoming traffic. Her car was hit on the passenger's side, and Shannon was thrown over Nikki and through the driver's side window. Shannon was pronounced dead at the scene.

Nikki sustained serious head and abdominal injuries that left her in a coma for six weeks. Her brother and his friends had minor injuries and were released from the hospital after a short stay.

Since our school was only a half mile away, and since we had just been dismissed for the day, news traveled quickly back to the school. I was in yearbook photography and cheerleading, so I was still on campus for practice and to work on photos. I was developing prints in the darkroom when a friend came in and told me the school officials needed to talk with me outside. I asked her if Shannon was okay, and that's when she told me what had happened.

At first I couldn't understand what she was saying—it seemed unreal. Then it hit me, and I lost it. I crumpled to the ground and cried uncontrollably.

I couldn't believe it. We went to the scene of the accident, but it was all blocked off, and they were not letting anyone through. We went to the hospital, hoping Shannon might be there. And that's when it was confirmed: Shannon had never been brought there because she was dead.

The accident happened on a Thursday, and Shannon's funeral was set for Monday afternoon at 1:00. The school let students leave if they wanted to go to the funeral, and five hundred of us went. I didn't return to school until Wednesday, two days after the funeral.

Shannon and I had shared a locker, and when I opened it that first time back, I sobbed. The school administrators had taken her personal items and some of the school's books, but they left the stuff we used to decorate the inside of our locker, including the picture of Shannon with her first car, a red Honda Prelude that her parents had just bought for her.

I squatted down and buried my face in my locker so nobody would see me crying so hard. I was always crying. I didn't know how to deal with the emotions I was feeling. The staff got us cheerleaders together to talk through how we were feeling and to find out who our support system was. I was so depressed that I almost quit cheerleading that day.

The guy I was starting to date fell off the face of the earth, not knowing how to deal with such a big thing. I felt like I could talk to my mom about how I was feeling and to my oldest brother, but since they'd never experienced such a personal death before, there was almost always something they didn't understand about it all. They did all they could to be there, but I eventually stopped talking about it because I didn't know what to do. My mom sent me to a counselor a few times, but they just told me I was grieving and it would take some time to feel better. I felt like I had lost everything good in my life and didn't know how to feel better.

I was broken.

Then a girl in Yearbook Photography class, Jennifer, started talking to me. She was fun to talk with; she got my mind off things and always had fun stories about people she knew and things she was involved in. We started talking more in class and went to the mall to hang out. We hit it off so well the first time we hung out that, from that moment on, we were nearly inseparable.

We always talked about how we wished we would have known each other early on in high school because we would have had so much fun. She talked to me a lot about Shannon and how I was feeling. I always felt like I was the information center for everyone at school on the progress of Nikki's recovery, but Jennifer would always ask me how *I* was doing, not just how Nikki was doing.

Jennifer was there in a noninvasive way, talking to me about death and life and spiritual things. She invited me over to her house, and I got to know her parents very well. I started to find comfort in them, and that led to my asking a lot of questions about God and who he was.

Soon I was going with Jennifer to her youth group when I could and to church on Sundays with her and her family. I ended up taking a class for new believers at the church that explained who Jesus really was and how to become a follower. After the class I felt ready to make a decision to follow Jesus. I wanted to learn more about being baptized as well. They talked about baptism being an outward profession of an inward decision that I was wanting to make.

> **Jennifer was there in a noninvasive way, talking to me about death and life and spiritual things.**

We had graduated by then, and while I stayed home to work and save for school, Jennifer had gone away to school in California and was halfway through her freshman year at a Bible college. When she came back home for her winter break, she baptized me at the church. It was a special time I will never forget. It was on that day that I decided to follow Jesus and announce that decision to my friends and family as well.

I was at peace that day as I went to Jen's parents' house for lunch afterward. We reflected on how my year had gone from tragedy to Jesus. Jennifer and her parents convinced me to join her in California so I could take Bible classes.

Soon enough I made it to California and reunited with my best friend. We had a great time in college together. We connected on a deep level. I knew that God had brought us together, and I was blessed to have a friend who really understood me. I never thought of Jennifer as a replacement for Shannon. I was just blown away that God would care about me enough to bring Jennifer along.

We have known each other for almost sixteen years now, the longest friendship I have ever had. She was my maid of honor, and I was her matron of honor just last year. I sometimes think about how different my life would have been if Jennifer hadn't made that first contact, taken that first step in becoming my friend. She knew I needed Jesus and a friend in my life. She was obedient to that and jumped right in. She is like family, and no matter how different our lives have become, she is and always will be my best friend. I don't understand why we experience brokenness. Some situations like these never will make much sense to me. I did learn through this that Jesus loves the broken. It is times like these that Jesus seems to show up, and he sure did in my life through a friend named Jen.

Unexpected Pain

In my travels and my line of work, I have met some great people. Every Sunday after speaking at a different church, as soon as I exit the stage I am usually met by a woman who will begin to weep. More times than not, they will begin to tell me about how they have lost their spouse because of a sexual addition or pornography addiction. I will try to comfort them or find someone from the church who will hold them and just pray with them.

Pain is no respecter of persons. Jeanette and I have a friend, Jack. He is an author and musician who knows a thing or two about being broken. Over the course of a three-year marriage, Jack's wife cheated on him twice, once with a good friend of his—a man whom she is now planning to marry.

Jack found out about the second affair when he logged onto his wife's instant messaging account and was almost immediately greeted with completely inappropriate messages by a man who obviously thought Jack's wife had logged on. When he confronted her about it, she showed no remorse or acknowledgment of wrongdoing. She just wanted out of the marriage, and she didn't care about breaking Jack's heart to do it.

In that moment of learning about his wife's indecency, Jack's heart had to have died.

That's why Jack reminds me of Lazarus. In the book of John, chapter 11, a man named Lazarus got sick and died. There is a story about the girl who wiped perfume on Jesus' feet with her hair—this guy was her brother. He died, they buried him, and then Jesus showed up four days later.

And Mary, the sister, said to him, "Why didn't you prevent this? We're in a lot of pain here, and if you'd been around, this wouldn't have happened."

How many of us, in times of brokenness, have said that to Jesus? Or if not Jesus, then God, or whatever deity happened to be convenient? "Why did you let this happen?"

Regardless of the accusations leveled against him, Jesus doesn't let it get to him. In fact, when he saw Mary crying, he started crying too.

Jesus weeps with the broken, even when he knows things we don't. He sees things from a different perspective, but he *understands* the perspective of the broken person, he knows how that feels, and he weeps right along with them.

But he doesn't address his accusers. He doesn't defend himself. He just goes to the tomb, has them roll the stone away, and hollers into the cave: "Lazarus! Get out here!"

And there he is: Lazarus, strolling forward, resurrected.

Jesus weeps with the broken, even when he knows things we don't.

I'm simplifying things here, but in the midst of Jack's brokenness, he felt dead. Then Jesus stepped in, wept with him, and called out to his heart: "Come back to life!"

Jack has since forgiven his wife and her new lover. It's still tough on him, and he has a ways to go, of course; but through it all, he knows that Jesus is right there, weeping with him.

Diagnosed with Death

Another story of brokenness illustrates the miraculous healing power of God.

In 1993 Sue's husband left her. Alone, barreling toward midlife, and desperate to take care of her children, Sue began to date.

After their first meeting, Sue thought Donald was a great guy. He looked kind. He had a great job. The profile seemed safe. Sue and Donald began dating regularly, and the relationship became intimate.

Everything was looking up. Sue's wounds from her previous marriage began to heal, and with a little help from Donald, she was able to take care of her children.

All that changed when the blood bank called less than a month after she donated. They demanded a meeting with her. "Susan, why did you give blood?" they asked. "How many times have you given blood since you were here last time?" the questioner barked. Sue was confused. Within a few minutes, Sue was told she was HIV positive.

"I tried to figure it out," recounted Sue, whom I met through a friend. "I knew the only person I had been with since my husband was Donald." Broken in tone and in spirit, Sue described the pain of her past.

"When they told me I had HIV, a thousand thoughts went through my head. I felt like I had been diagnosed with death."

Sue confronted Donald, and he admitted his mistake. Sue could have walked away from him forever, and everyone around her would have understood. But after several conversations, she chose the harder path. Sue forgave Donald.

"Together we tried to put life back together."

No one outside the family knew their situation. Sue thought her church would help her. Unfortunately, she could not find the courage to tell them. She'd heard subtle comments that AIDS was a curse for sin. Some in their ignorance spoke of AIDS as a gay disease. Some spoke of it as being the penalty for sin. Internally broken with HIV, spiritually depleted, and imprisoned by silence, Sue chose to care for Donald alone as his disease progressed.

"There were many days where it was only me and God," she told me. "Donald was dying, and I was trying to care for the man who infected me. I wanted him to know Jesus the way I did. The only way he would get it would be to see it.

Jesus cared for the broken, and I had to see to it that Donald died in dignity."

A few weeks before his last breath, Sue communicated Jesus' love to Donald. He believed it because he saw Sue live it.

After several conversations, she chose the harder path. Sue forgave Donald.

Immediately after her diagnosis, the doctors had given Sue three years to live. Today, nearly sixteen years later, Sue is remarried and is leading a healthy life. Some give the credit for her survival to the antiretroviral cocktail (HIV/AIDS Suppression Medicine) that she takes daily, but Sue thinks otherwise.

"I believe my life's longevity is the result of knowing that Jesus reached out and loved me when I was unlovely. I believe he took my brokenness and made it whole."

A Prescription

Jeanette was broken from the loss a friend. Jack was crushed because of betrayal. Sue's world shattered because of a series of decisions. They each saw some form of death, but each also witnessed some kind of resurrection.

The prescription for brokenness is Jesus. He is a master at molding people back to life. Scripture makes it clear that we are all broken. No one is immune. But in Christ we can find hope and wholeness.

Consider reading just a few stories from the Bible that illustrate Jesus' ability to bring wholeness to broken people in broken situations:

John 8:1–11: A woman is caught in adultery and faces public execution.

Matthew 20:29–34: Two blind men beg on the side of the road.

Mark 5:35–43: Jairus loses all hope when his daughter dies.

Allow Jesus to walk alongside you. Allow him to bring hope and help. Allow what was shattered to be made whole.

Craig

We sat motionless, having just heard Israel Houghton rip through a set of high octane music at the Dream It Conference in Sacramento. It helped that Jason had clued me in to his music. I don't listen to much Christian music, but something was different about Israel. I saw and heard a measure of realism and authenticity that gripped me. I sat stunned and wondered aloud who this guy was and where he came from. Jason replied that Israel was a driving force for the explosion of growth that had occurred at "Joel's."

Jason does this often. He gives me fragments of thought and assumes I know what he is saying. I know five people named Joel; apparently, one of them knew Israel. Jason wanted me to connect the dots.

By then the music soared to another level while Israel's band, New Breed, interacted with the crowd. Still waiting for Jason to finish the description of this particular Joel, I was confused.

Finally Jason connected the dots for me. "Israel is the worship leader at Lakewood Christian Church in Houston, Texas. Joel Osteen is the pastor. They worship at an NBA arena with 30,000 people each Sunday."

Oh. *That* Joel. He had my attention. I knew who Joel Osteen was. (I had seen his ministry on TV, and I had friends who had read *Your Best Life Now*, Joel's bestseller. I then added Joel and his lovely wife Victoria as a friend on Facebook. Now, we are best of friends. Well, not really—just Facebook friends.)

Jason was an obvious fan and admirer of Israel. After what I saw that night, I was too. He moved me like few had. By nature I am a mellow guy. I come from a traditional church that didn't worship with outward expressions or gestures. And the church I grew up in didn't allow drums. Jason, on the other hand—he's from a church like Israel's. I have watched Jason jump, sing, and really go for it in worship. That's just not me. But something was different about Israel. Authentic. Real. Hungering. Deep.

That stuck with me long after the night concluded.

A few weeks passed, and a friend and I connected for dinner. He did some of the promotion work for Dream It, and he talked about his love for Israel and his music. The impact Israel had on us was the centerpiece of our conversation. I asked him where the passion and energy came from, and he described how he had met Israel about a month before the conference. My friend was asked to go to a local venue and get a brief interview with Israel to use in promoting the conference.

He interviewed Israel about life, music, producing, Joel, and so much more. And toward the end of the interview, my friend discovered more than your typical interview reveals: Jesus loves the forgotten.

Israel described how his life nearly came to an end before it ever started. Deep within the belly of a seventeen-year-old Iowa girl beat the heart of a worshiper. But being white and pregnant with a black man's baby in the early 1970s was a bleak proposition. Pressured to abort, Israel's mother ran away.

"My mother is white," Israel recounted. "My biological father is black. When my mother was 17, she got pregnant. They lived in Waterloo, Iowa, which at the time in 1971 was a very segregated society. She came home and told her parents, 'I'm pregnant and the father is black.' They had a really difficult time with it."[1]

Israel was calm and very honoring when he described his mother's plight.

"I really should have been one of those abortion statistics you read about. . . . Her family wasn't supportive of their relationship and gave her the choice to have a back-alley abortion or to be disowned.[2]

> **"I really should have been one of those abortion statistics you read about."**

"The suggestion was, 'Have an abortion. Move on with your life.' She was a terrific concert pianist, she had everything ahead of her, and in a lot of ways had every reason to go, 'Let's just chalk this up as a mistake and move on.' She said, 'No, no, I'm going to keep this baby.' She ended up kind of getting shunned for a good chunk of her life after that and didn't have a lot of contact with her parents.[3]

"I'm here because of the decision she made—and because of her conversion shortly after that."[4]

Not Forgotten

The portable video lights raised the temperature in the room. The camera zoomed in while Israel told of his mother's experience of accepting Christ. While telling the story, he referenced the faithful love of God, who reaches for those who are forgotten in society, including his mom. God found his mother with an unborn child in her womb.

She was young, eight months pregnant, and alone. The biological father had left. Her parents had abandoned her. Now, living in Southern California, the question of what to do plagued her every day. Southern California had not forgotten the Watts Race Riots of the sixties. Few cared to see a white girl carrying a biracial child.

His story continues. The state of California would have taken him away from her "because she was considered an unfit mother, and she was on drugs. It was like the perfect *Lifetime* movie."[5]

But God had not forgotten.

Standing on the sidewalk near the corner of Carlsbad Avenue in San Diego, she was approached by a car pulling over to the gutter. Out of the blue, prompted by God, a complete stranger rolled down the window and spoke. She listened, and death was derailed.

His mother listened intently to the words of the woman in the car. She spoke with clarity and courage: "I don't know you, and I don't want to give you a hard time, but I was driving by and I really felt that I needed to come tell you Jesus loves you. You're not forgotten. You did the right thing. It's going to be all right."

Jesus loves the forgotten.

"Those words of life were so powerful to her and so revolutionary to her . . . that she got on her knees and gave her life to Jesus. I'm here today because of that woman's faithfulness to God to share the gospel with my mother."[6]

My friend and I were done eating. We reflected on how the pain of Israel's past propelled his music. As a tribute to the Truth that rescued his troubled, teenaged mom, Israel and his wife penned these words in a song: "I am not forgotten, God knows my name." The last stanza repeats the message: "I am not forgotten, never forsaken."[7] Sometimes I need to remember that. Do you?

We live in a fast-paced culture. The hustle and bustle of daily living mounts a constant pressure to get ahead, yet we never define what that means. Essentially, we are taught from the earliest age that the front of the line is the best. We are taught to step over or on top of others to get ours. Most parents mean well. They tell little Johnnie to be a "go-getter," but a go-getter is one who takes.

Along that trail, we can pass up people who need a smile, a word of hope, a lasting shoulder to lean on. And to stop on the Go-Getter Trail means we get passed up or passed over. That promotion at work rarely goes to the kindest or most compassionate employee. The caring often get kicked and stepped on.

The root of a multitude of social ills stems from one factor: so many are consumed with their world that they forget about others. Those others who need to see hope, friendship, and lasting compassion.

Many who get abortions do so because of bad advice that convinced them their future would be inconvenienced if they allowed life to continue. I am not talking as a political pundit about life or choice. I am talking about remembering the forgotten—not just the child, but the mom as well.

I have met with women in post-abortion conditions. Often, fear drove them to the clinic. They were consumed with the fear that they would not be able to take care of the child. But when I pressed on this, we would often

> **We are taught from the earliest age that the front of the line is the best.**

find that their fear was really discouragement disguised. They admitted they felt no one would be there to help them.

They were afraid they would be forgotten.

In day-to-day situations, even when people seek out hope or help, they are often forgotten. Consider this:

> The New York City medical examiner says a woman who died unnoticed on a Brooklyn hospital floor was killed by blood clots caused by a long period of physical inactivity. Esmin Green had been sitting in a waiting room at the Kings County Hospital Center for nearly 24 hours when she collapsed from her chair and slowly died on June 19. She lay on the floor for an hour before a nurse finally checked her pulse.[8]

She had been forgotten.

Have you ever been forgotten? Have you ever needed someone to talk to and been alone? Maybe you weren't considering abortion. Maybe you sought healing and hope and were unnoticed.

Maybe you've been forgotten by society.

Maybe you're a loner.

Growing tired of the pain, the forgotten become despondent.

But Jesus loves the forgotten.

Birthday Parties and Paramedics

Jesus was intentional about making a beeline to get his arms around the forgotten. Jesus chased them. Matthew 18:12 describes it this way, using sheep as an illustration: "What do you think? If a man owns a hundred sheep, and one of them wanders away, will he not leave the ninety-nine on the hills and go to look for the one that wandered off?"

Jesus loves the forgotten and the marginalized. He is committed to loving them through the disastrous, deadly, self-worth-eliminating effects of being overlooked.

On a long drive to Los Angeles, my friend Russ told me a story of the forgotten and how it changed the way he lived his life. In 1995, when he was a youth pastor, a group of students gathered for a birthday party at a local swimming hole, a small lake. He had just finished a series of talks with the group on practicing inclusion, and to put some practical action in play, he challenged everyone to invite people to join them on the journey called life. They started by giving an open invitation to a birthday celebration. The swimming party was informal, but it seemed everyone wanted to go.

By the end of the week, a student named Jerrod* had committed to go. Up until this point, his involvement in the youth group had been nominal at best. Jerrod was tall and lanky, with stringy, dark hair. His parents were older and exceptionally smart, and he had inherited their intelligence.

Jerrod excelled in school. Advanced Placement courses with all A's made social connections in our group of good but not staggeringly brilliant students difficult. His asthmatic condition ruled out sports, so his social outlets were few and far between. Yet active members Tommy and Mike were committed to getting Jerrod to connect. The swimming party would be a great first step. They invited him, and Jerrod decided to go.

> **Jesus loves the forgotten and the marginalized. He is committed to loving them through the disastrous, deadly, self-worth-eliminating effects of being overlooked.**

The parking lot at the swimming hole began to fill with high school and some college kids. Music pumped, and the group of forty began to swim and jump off the floating pontoon that made the lake a favorite social place. Even Jerrod laid out a towel and flirted with getting into the water. As Russ described the party at the lake, his voice crackled. Despite it being more than a decade ago, it seemed the pain was still close.

Russ cleared his throat and continued explaining. He said that after a half hour of prompting, Jerrod waded in. No one commented on his ghostly white legs and farmer-tanned

* Names have been changed to protect the families that still deal with the daily pain of this episode.

arms; they were just glad he was there. Finally, in a courageous lunge, Jerrod dog paddled out to the floating island and some of the students helped him climb out of the water. The swim platform was warmed from the afternoon sun. Jerrod laughed. Others laughed with him and had to remind him to take his swim goggles off his eyes while standing atop the pontoon.

After nearly an hour, some of those who had brought the food and birthday cake came out of the small lake house and hollered to the swimmers to come on up and get some cake. One after another, the confident leaped into the lake off the floating platform. Horseplay ensued on the way to the shore. Yet still standing on the pontoon was Jerrod.

As the beach quickly cleared, Jerrod's towel was the only one left. He had been forgotten. Nobody remembers him calling out. I imagined he did not want to seem high maintenance; after all, this was his first time out.

The partygoers finished off the cake. Others laughed and joked. Soon the mess was cleaned up, and one by one the parking lot emptied. No one noticed that Jerrod's car was still there. Had anyone looked down on the beach, they would have seen his towel still laid out, meticulously placed without a wrinkle. That is how he left it.

Near midnight, Russ's church pager went off with a 911 code. Quickly he called into the church system and heard the voice of a calm but concerned mother.

"Hello, this is Jerrod's mom. He has yet to come home from the swim party. Maybe he forgot to call. Please call me if he is with you."

Hearing his mom's voice on the phone sent Russ's mind into overdrive.

Again choked, Russ paused, his tone subsided.

"I concluded he must have left the party with one of his new friends. Within an hour I had gotten ready, picked up one of my youth leaders, and headed out to Jerrod's house."

Jerrod lived in a beautiful home with his folks. The gated community was only two or three miles from where the swimming hole party had occurred. As Russ walked into their home, concern gripped him. Jerrod's mother had moved from patience to panic. It was after midnight.

The only thing Russ could think to do was call the police and then head to the swimming hole. Jerrod's dad offered to go, so they loaded into the family car and drove the short distance.

It was ominous, to say the least. The car's headlights reflected off the lake.

"When I pulled up, a warm, humid mist hovered over the water. It seemed like a movie. In moments, it became the worst kind of horror imaginable." Russ was fully engaged in describing this life-changing event.

Scurrying ahead of the young man's dad, Russ asked him to go look near the building to see if Jerrod had left a note. He knew there wouldn't be one, but he didn't want his dad to go down to the lake's edge with him.

What if Jerrod was lying there? What if his body was floating? Every worst-case scenario sprinted through Russ's mind.

Russ quickly jogged the fifty-yard distance from the car to the small sandy beach. He saw the towel spread out. It was right where Jerrod had left it. In the dark, but notice-able from the idling car's headlights, a small five-inch-square bump the size of a wallet protruded from under the towel. A quick feel to the right of Jerrod's wallet revealed the keys to his dad's car.

Russ scurried back to the family car, where Jerrod's dad waited. Through the darkness, the father saw his car in the corner of the gravel lot—the car his son had borrowed. The reality that something was seriously wrong set in. They left everything alone. Russ described how he wanted to believe Jerrod had gone with friends and would come back to get his car. But as they backed out of the lot in the summer dark-ness, hope evaporated as their worst fears formed.

The next morning the sun rose and *the forgotten* was found. The family, Russ, and two detectives arrived back at the lake. By now the underwater dive team from the sheriff's office had strewn crime tape around the end of the lake where the party was held. The pontoon became a makeshift crime lab. Seeing the family and their initial shock at the commotion, the detective pulled Russ aside and explained that until they obtained some ideas or leads, it needed to be treated like a potential crime scene. What separated it from a typical case where a teen just didn't come home was that the towel, wal-let, and keys had been found. If Jerrod had decided to take off, he would have grabbed his wallet at the very least.

As the detective concluded, Russ was making his own discovery—the discovery of what death looked like up close. While the cop talked, Russ's eyes drifted to the div-ers swimming in the water. They made a search team grid, first focusing on the area between the floating platform and the beach in line with the laid-out towel. In less than ten minutes, the divers floated a stationary buoy. It floated directly above the place where they had found something. The divers climbed out of the water and consulted the lead detective. He motioned to the chaplain on site, and the two walked to those waiting in the lake house.

Jerrod had been found.

The coroner explained later that Jerrod drowned due to a possible asthma attack while swimming. Nothing could have been done to save him—he was alone. Then came the questions, questions for which Russ had no answers:

Why didn't anyone see him?

Why was he alone?

Why was he overlooked?

How was he forgotten?

Raw Regret

Days later, Jerrod's school postponed classes for his funeral. One by one, students lined up to talk. Some wept as they offered condolences to the family. Others tried to say they were close to Jerrod. They weren't. He was forgotten.

"It was the hardest day I have had as a youth pastor." Russ wiped the tears from his eyes. His regret was raw.

All I could do was wish it had been different.

"I kept replaying the tape in my mind. The group must have quickly swum in to get some cake and celebrate. I understand. I just wished that someone would have remembered Jerrod." Emotion now caused Russ to stop for a moment to regain his composure.

"In my mind, I see him pacing back and forth, trapped on this man-made island. As everyone dove in, Jerrod was forgotten."

As Russ stopped speaking, I continued to drive. Thoughts consumed me of how it could be different. Jesus finds, not forgets. We live in a world where many of us are in the same boat—or to better phrase it, without a boat. We are trapped alone on a man-made island called Forgotten. We walk through life with nothing more than surface conversations. I have had days where the self-imposed depth of my human interaction occurred at a drive-thru; I quickly sped past some people with as little connection as possible. Others were banished or mandated into the slavery of solitude.

While Russ spoke, it seemed as if he were still processing the fallout by replaying it in his mind.

"Jerrod had put his goggles back on. When I had to identify the body, they were on. Even now my mind flashes to his final moments. His thin, weak body pacing back and forth just a hundred feet away from where he could see everything he wanted." Russ was done. The story was over. I finished it with a conversation in my mind.

In his final minutes, before he would stand comforted by the King of Creation, Jerrod must have thought that the thing he came for had escaped him.

For years Russ has been pummeled by the irony. As a youth pastor, he constantly pushed people to remember the forgotten. He implored them to practice inclusion. Yet, in doing that very thing, Jerrod ended up at a party where he was forgotten and overlooked.

Have you ever felt forgotten or overlooked? I have. I constantly fight the insecurities and feelings of rejection. I feel forgotten, but I am hopeful.

We, the forgotten—we are children of the King.

Maybe you feel forgotten. Maybe it is not abortion. Maybe it is not abandonment. Maybe it is not addiction. It doesn't matter—forgotten is forgotten. But whatever got you to that place was remedied. We are hopeful.

The flip side of that coin is to take a practical look around you and see if there are people in isolation around you. Reach out to them the way Jesus would. Only Jesus can bring one back into Hope. Jesus loves the forgotten.

> **That is what Jesus does. He brings purpose out of pain. He brings life through death.**

That is what Jesus does. He brings purpose out of pain. He brings life through death.

Jerrod, in your death, you are remembered. You are not forgotten.

1. Kristi Watts and Julie Blim, "Israel Houghton: An Intimate Portrait of Worship," cbnmusic.com, http://www.cbn.com/cbnmusic/Interviews/700club_IsraelHoughton_041205.aspx.

2. LaTonya Taylor, "A Friend of God," ChristianMusicToday.com, http://www.christianitytoday.com/music/interviews/2004/israelhoughton-0904.html.

3. Watts and Blim, "Israel Houghton."

4. Taylor, "Friend of God."

5. Watts and Blim, "Israel Houghton."

6. Ibid.

7. Israel Houghton and Aaron Lindsey, "Not Forgotten," Integrity, 2005.

8. Associated Press, June 11, 2008.

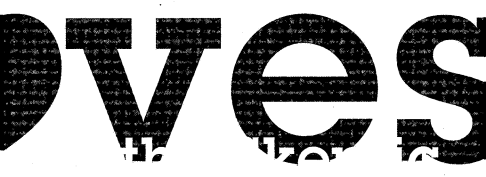

Jason

I have a penchant for problems. They find me. I draw madness like a magnet, often finding myself talking to people who don't think, look, act, or believe like me. It makes life interesting.

The people are not the problem. The problem is getting them to sit down and talk rationally. Many times, once people find out what I believe, they decide to have a debate instead of a dialogue. I am not a debater. I am a discusser. I like to talk over what they think, especially about things that matter to me.

It makes for strange conversations over cups of coffee. Just days ago, I had one of these coffee times with my friend Keith. He is an atheist. And a funny one. In fact, Keith is a comedian who created a comedy tour called Coexist Comedy. It features four stand-up comics: a Muslim, a Christian, a Jew, and Keith. They cram themselves into one van and hit the road, going to many different venues. It isn't a stretch to think that much of their material is birthed on these road trips.

Each comic in the van has a different perspective of Jesus: a good teacher, a Savior, a prophet, a person. Even Keith concedes that Jesus was a person.

I should explain how I met Keith the Atheist. And I will. But before I do, let me explain my firsthand knowledge of the weird reactions that the simple message of Jesus can stir up.

A few years ago, I was walking down a street in Santa Rosa, California, flanked by some teenage students from a group I was mentoring. We had driven over to Santa Rosa to spend a Saturday afternoon walking through some of the quaint shops. We often took these kinds of day trips to curb boredom, and they always ended up presenting an incredible life lesson or two.

Maybe I should have been a sociologist, because I love to watch people. As we strolled up and down the streets of this small Northern California town, I took in the cross-section of people. Young couples in daydreamy love held hands as they walked in the town square; married couples from nearby towns cruised in their convertibles on wine-tasting excursions; antique hunters searched for the once-in-a-lifetime treasure hidden on a dusty shelf. The locals lined the small town center to watch the people from afar flood their small economy. Some senior citizens smiled in the delight of the sunlight. Others looked frustrated by the teens who skated the curbs.

A group of local teens became submerged in a game of hacky sack, kicking the beanbag from foot to foot. They were dressed head-to-toe in hippie apparel that made them look like they were stuck in a '60s commune.

A hemp necklace, dreads, a tie-dyed shirt, and a lip ring were what got my attention first. She was walking toward us. Alone, with a backpack in tow, a smile on her face. She squinted her eyes into the midafternoon sunlight. As she approached, I lost track of what the kids in my group were doing.

As she got closer, I noticed her smile began to fade. The kids, as I affectionately had begun to call my students, were engaged in some whistled form of "Name That Tune," and this now-frowning young lady was listening in. It wasn't long before she expressed her agitation.

"I hate that song!"

Stunned, I searched my mind for a couple of things. First, I tried to figure out how someone who looked so sweet could sound so mean and angry. Her words had a wounded edge to them. Then I tried to figure out what song she was referring to.

My whistling kids had laid down the mono track of "Jesus Loves Me." Walking down the street, one of our girls had absentmindedly broken out an oldie.

> Jesus loves me, this I know,
> for the Bible tells me so.

By now I had put a couple of the puzzle pieces together. This hippie girl looked like she was poised for a fight right there on the street. Her hands were firmly pressed against her hips, while her feet, shoulder-width apart, were firmly planted. Her right foot tapped the pavement, impatiently demanding a response from me.

ls
oves

Her lip was pierced with a hoop. It appeared that her tongue was fluttering back and forth on the inside of her piercing, a nervous twitch that added to the picture of her agitation.

"You hate the kids' song she whistled?" I said, as softly, slowly, and graciously as I could. I treated the conversation like I was walking on verbal egg shells.

She blasted back without a moment of reflection. "I hate the song, and I hate the people who sing it!"

By now, the students with me had stopped all movement and honed in on this situation, thinking perhaps that this hippie girl was about to beat me.

Still tapping. Still twitching.

A crowd of ten or so people began to gather, watching our exchange.

She was hunkered down and ready, waiting for a fight. I toyed with charmingly pointing out her error: she stated that she hated the people who *sang* that song, but it had clearly been *whistled*.

I bit my lip, though. Finally, after what seemed like hours (but was only a few seconds), I probed for a deeper assessment. "What's wrong with the song?"

"I think it's a lie!" Her tone had softened. Maybe she was shocked at the quietness of my response.

Then she huffed off, shoving through the crowd. That's it. No explanation. No dialogue. She simply thought it was a lie.

Somehow, somewhere, to that girl, the wheels came off the story behind that song. I thought she was too young to have such an angry, emotional response to the thought of

"Jesus loves you" has become an overstated Christian cliché.

Jesus' love. I wished I could talk to her about it, but I never saw her again.

It really rattled me. Not as a self-proclaimed and unlearned sociologist, but as a person who is interested in other people's perspectives on faith.

Whether the statement is spoken *to* me or *by* me, "Jesus loves me" and "Jesus loves you" express a simple idea that holds very little clout with many in global culture.

" 'The Bible tells me so' isn't enough," some would say. "There has to be more. Sure, I can start with scripture as a compass, but I want to read the Jesus of scripture in action."

"Jesus loves you" has become an overstated Christian cliché from the religious establishment. What was once meant to be a statement of concern, a thought, or a pronouncement of spiritual enlightenment has been reduced to a casual exchange in passing.

Jesus Loves You.

Overused and often nothing more than trite Christianese, the statement has lost its punch. I've seen shoppers at Christmas drop a quarter or two into the bell-shaker's red bucket and say, "Jesus loves you." It is almost as bad as "He's the reason for the season." Before the coin hits the bottom of the bucket, they're on their way. Maybe they believe that speaking those words is enough to cure the social ills of society. But the statement alone is just that—an empty statement. The real impact comes in showing them the Jesus who is the life behind the statement—*he* is what can change the world.

The Real Jesus

Many in today's culture were raised without a working knowledge of the historical figure of Jesus. The closest exposure they had to him was hearing his name as part of a frustrated exclamation.

For many, the name "Jesus" summons feelings and thoughts of disillusionment. It even conjures questions that many can't or won't answer. My hope is that, since you're holding this little book, there may be something stirring within you.

What do you think?

Is Jesus real? Or is he a myth?

Was Jesus just a good person? Or was he who he said he was?

Was Jesus like every other religious leader? Or is there something different about him?

What do you think about Jesus? Have you considered who he was or what his purpose was? Have you ever wondered why he lived his life the way he did? Why history describes him as consumed by love?

Jesus expressed love through action. His ministry was more than, "Hey, I love you." It was expressed with the attitude, "Hey, what can I do to *show* you that I love you?" We have only a brief mention of him saying "I love you," but those around Jesus got it.[1] They got it to the point of death.

A Jewish historian named Josephus recorded that eleven of Jesus' twelve disciples died as martyrs in allegiance to the love they understood from Jesus. It was a type of unconditional love that was available for every person on the planet. It was and still is inclusive. It was and still is illogical and goes completely against the grain of culture. Josephus was not a Christian, but he was amazed by the model life of selflessness that Jesus led.

The religious people were interested in enforcing rules and judging those who didn't keep them. They hated Jesus. They spoke of a belief system so dogmatic that it became irrelevant to the majority of the population. The culture of Jesus' time was filled with exclusivity, and the religious leaders hated Jesus because he rebelled against that. He was snuffed out for practicing inclusion of the outcast and lowly.

The culture of our time, however, is largely *not* religious and has become indifferent toward him. Having spoken to thousands of people about their perspectives, I can tell you: a lot of people have painted Jesus with a broad brush that often distorts who he was.

A vast majority of American culture recognizes Jesus as an iconic symbol. This recognition has created a renewal in Jesus imagery. Yet much of the time it has little, if anything, to do with spirituality—it's just trendy. A few years ago, celebrities from Ashton Kutcher to Paris Hilton sported "Jesus Is My Homeboy" shirts everywhere in Southern California.

The image of the real Jesus either draws or repels. There is hardly any middle ground. Some embrace everything he did. Others think he was an elevated folk hero. Jesus is polarizing.

Maybe everything you heard about Jesus can or should be redefined.

Maybe everything you thought about Jesus was the result of religion and dogma.

Maybe the things you hate or love about him were defined *for* you because of what you were told growing up.

To think that Jesus loves unconditionally would mean that he has to look past all my faults, my failures, my mistakes. Looking back over my life, it's hard to believe Jesus could do that.

And that's what I am saying. If Jesus can love me, he can also love *you*. Imagine that. *Jesus loves you.* Many struggle to grasp the thought of Jesus loving us, thinking of him as some inanimate object or some mystical presence, floating out in space like a distant Cupid, sprinkling love over society. No. Jesus' love is a reality—a life-changing, *world*-changing reality.

Jesus demonstrated that in order to be first, we must become comfortable with last place. To be strong, we must display meekness; to be valued, give rather than get. Offer people a seat at the table of inclusion. Love others, no matter their status. The social outcast, the sick, the dejected, the afflicted, the broken, the hurting, the abandoned—Jesus loved them all. Regardless of where a person landed on the cultural ladder, Jesus' value for them never wavered.

Jesus loves people. From porn stars to pastors; from soccer moms to shysters. Jesus loves liars, thieves, prostitutes, embezzlers, prisoners—all of humanity. He loves those who believe and those who don't. This is the good news of the gospel.

> **Regardless of where a person landed on the cultural ladder, Jesus' value for them never wavered.**

Atheist Panhandler Keith

Last year on a cold Sunday morning, a friend of mine walked over to me in the lobby of our church. It seemed the church I attend had become the target of a picketer and film crew. This is nothing new to us. Capital Christian Center is a highly visible church on a main highway, and in years past, when people want to make a statement about God, they picket us. It's totally illogical. People show up with their signs and make their statement. I enjoy talking to them, even when they hate me or what I believe, which is much of the time. Mostly, the picketers are fringe religious groups that think our message of love and hope is too inclusive and not judgmental. Yes, illogical. When I heard it was not the normal picketers, I was intrigued.

As I walked to the edge of our property, the first thing I noticed about this thin man in his mid-twenties was the sign he carried. "Atheist: Will Convert For Food!" I greeted him with a grin.

His name was Keith.

"Hey, my name's Jason. Can I help you with anything?" I was sincere in my tone.

"Nah, just an atheist who will convert to Christianity for some food." Keith could not hide a small, sheepish grin.

Over the course of a long dialogue, I found out that Keith, a confessed skeptic and frequent contributor to atheist conversation, was hardly willing to convert for food. He had made a local game out of standing on street corners with a panhandling sign that read "Why Lie? I Need A Drink."

See? Funny. At least to Keith.

He told me his story. He was raised in a family that had a knowledge and respect for God. But somewhere along the way, he became disillusioned by the hypocrisy he saw in the Christians around him, which eventually led him to my church, where he'd come to bait Christians into a debate that he could catch on video to post or blog. After thirty minutes of attempting to talk with those leaving the church, Keith had been told in one way or another that he was loved. Few words were spoken to him, but the essence in both words and actions was to communicate one thing: Jesus loves the skeptic.

In the brisk November air, Keith and I talked for over an hour. When we finished, he told me he was going to post a blog about our conversation on his website. I rushed home that day to see what he said . . . or better yet, what he thought I had said. Here it is, exactly the way he posted it:

I've long hated Capital Christian Center. Why? Well, because, um, you see, they're big and they're part of the power structure, which is to say their congregation is made up of a bunch of well to do folks in nice SUVs, and their super visible, being right off the freeway and they have a big giant gold cross as a symbol.

I wanted to do the "Atheist. Please help, God Bless" sign for a long time, and I mentioned doing it there, at Capital Christian to John, who films me, thought it was a great idea and with his prodding it happened. I was somewhat reluctant because I don't like to engage people in a confrontational manner. Panhandling with a sign is pretty passive but taking it to them, on Sunday felt intentionally abrasive, and it probably was. I was wondering if I should just go back to my freeway off ramp. But now, we got up early, well early for Jonathon anyway, and we went to church.

Well, those Capital Christian jerks, they let me down. They didn't harass us or even make us leave their property. THEY BROUGHT ME COFFEE! A few of them gave me money, eleven bucks total. This of course [ticks] me off, it's not what I went there for.

John put a microphone on me and then hid in the bushes across from the church. They were spotted right away by the security truck. I was skating and waiting for church to let out, not flying my sign. John told the security guy that they were doing a documentary on graffiti, and were getting shots of the graffiti on the freeway signs.

People started exiting the church so I got in place and flew my sign. "Atheist. Please Help. God Bless" on one side, and "Atheist, Will convert for food. God Bless?" on the other. The security came to talk to me. They asked what I was doing and then they told me that they might have to direct people to a different entrance if traffic was being impeded by folks responding to me. I told them to let me know if it got to be a problem. I told them I was an artist trying to make a living panhandling so I could work on my writing and other art without having to work every day. They seemed to find this reasonable.

I lied to them about how closely affiliated with the film crew I was. For whatever reason, I felt like I might be allowed to stay longer if I said the film guys were into what I was doing so they just showed up in different places where I panhandled. I probably didn't have to lie.

I was talking with the two security guys, both of whom were volunteers and attended service at this church, when another parishioner drove up and asked if he could take me grocery shopping. I told him no thanks, that I was work-ing to get rent more than food.

I stayed there a while, and one of the security guys brought me a cup of coffee, which was actually really appreciated. I switched to another parking lot exit which was getting more traffic, but mostly I wanted to stand by myself to get a better feel for people's reactions. Most folks laughed, smiled, waved, and offered to pray for me. A few more folks gave me money. One of the security guys, Chris, came and asked me if I'd mind moving further down the street. I told him I'd really like to stay where I was and he let me. Then a young pastor came out and talked to me.

He had hip hair and a soul patch. He was dressed hip. He talked kind of hip, but he was pretty nice. His name is Jason. He didn't ask me to split and we just chatted about "god and man and law." I asked him my panhandling ques-tions "Do you think panhandling should be protected as free speech?" He did. "Do you give to panhandlers?" He does, but not cash. Food, and offers of places to stay or find work. I was increasingly uncomfortable with having someone with me; I really wanted to panhandle alone. I forgot to ask him if he believed in the affluent panhandler/scam-artist myth.

The guy who earlier had offered to take me grocery shopping came back and offered me five bucks and he gave me a coke. His name is Kevin and he's the nicest guy in the world. I couldn't take his five bucks. I told Kevin and Jason that I do this mostly to document how much I can make, and then I make money putting the stories on line and soliciting there from folks who know how desperate I am. I took the six bucks I'd made there and asked the pastor if they had a poor box. He said they did and he assured me that money in that box did not go to preaching at people but just to food programs. When I said goodbye Kevin gave me a big hug. Ha ha. What a sweetheart. Then I hugged the pastor.

So were they great folks or were they just really good PR people? Probably some of each. I'm sad that the money they collect every week is spent on big beautiful buildings and hip clothes, but I'm having trouble maintaining my judgemental attitude, and maybe I'll be more open to working with organizations like theirs, hopefully influencing what they do spend their money on. I am no Christian, and I'm sure I could find some homophobia and other such reasons to disagree with this church's policies, but I'm glad I accidentaly got confronted with the fact that they're just people like everyone else trying to be the best people they can be according to their beliefs.

A few weeks passed, and I emailed Keith. We connected for a coffee and continued to stay in contact. Essentially, Keith realized that sometimes the loudest cry of "Jesus loves you" doesn't have words connected to it. It can be a cup of coffee or, in Keith's case, a cup of tea. If we could only see how vital it is for us to connect and converse with skeptics. Jesus would.

That's what makes this story so profound to me. Jesus was hated by the religious because he spent his time with people like Keith and people like me. We are all the same to Jesus. We are all broken people who are flawed. I am flawed. Keith is flawed. You are flawed. We all are. These flaws have created insecurities and self-esteem issues. We have been taught that we have to fake it until we make it.

Brennan Manning, who wrote the classic book *The Ragamuffin Gospel*, is often attributed as the author of this quote:

"The greatest single cause of atheism in the world today is Christians who acknowledge Jesus with their lips, then walk out the door and deny him with their lifestyle. That is what an unbelieving world simply finds unbelievable."

So many times we ignore our need for God. We don't want to admit we have such a need, but it's there. He wants to mop up the mess(es) we have made. He wants to bring wholeness.

Everybody needs wholeness. Jesus' entire mission was love, to restore that which was wrong. The broken pain of humanity and its perplexities can be brought back into right standing.

In my experience, most skeptics' root issue is one of trust. They cannot, for whatever reason, trust the claims of Christ. They refuse to allow the spiritual aptitude of their intellect to engage in the abstract. If it is not provable or, some would even argue, visible, then it is not of value.

This lack of trust usually comes from the fact that they have been burned. Some religious person has failed or abused them. Rather than acknowledging it, the perpetrator (a pastor or priest, often) who represented "God-ordained" leadership" passed it off, was excused of horrible behavior, or was not confronted.

> "The greatest single cause of atheism in the world today is Christians who acknowledge Jesus with their lips, then walk out the door and deny him with their lifestyle. That is what an unbelieving world simply finds unbelievable."

Skepticism ensues.

Granted, this may only be one lens. I have not talked to every skeptic. But of the hundreds I have talked to, most have had an experience with the church. Of those I am in relationship with, many tell of how they were burnt or let down, judged for questioning something, or isolated because of their differences.

I don't know Keith's reason. He has not yet told me. Maybe he is afraid to. Yep, back to trust. As I have gotten to know him, I think part of it is just that he likes to argue and get people ticked. But I also think part of him wants to dodge the responsibility of giving credence to God, because if he did, he would then have to be responsible to God.

Whether you were raised in a Christian home or this is your first exposure to him, consider the thoughts, practices, and actions of Jesus. When I looked into these, I discovered something I wasn't expecting. He wasn't what I expected. He wasn't like the people who told me about him.

He didn't expect perfection. He looked for intention. He told the people who followed him that they should love the unlovely and that they should seek to be patient with those who were still in the process of discovery.

He was perfect for the skeptics.

Jesus for the Skeptic

When I was a skeptic, I scoured over as many historical snapshots of Jesus as I could get my hands on. I looked for something to present a clear understanding of who this man was. Throughout history, no other political, spiritual, or social leader had more impact than Jesus. Oddly, the skeptics in his day *were* the religious. Today, it's the other way around. But if Jesus' message has not changed, how did skepticism change camps?

Simple: the issue is not with Jesus.

I am not about to elaborate his résumé to build structural supports for a stage to introduce him. Instead, I am thinking of how this man made a statement that continues to produce change in those who consider it centuries later. To this day, I am intrigued; studying his interactions left me with more questions than answers.

How did a man who lived two thousand years ago gain eternal traction? Jesus was unknown until the age of thirty, when he began to speak more publicly. For the next thirty-six months, he traveled the dusty streets of the Middle East, communicating a message that was the opposite of what the culture taught. This message was engraved on people's hearts to the point of being willing to die, like he did, for his cause.

Some claimed he was a fortune-teller. He did tell the future. He predicted things and they came true.

Some claimed that he was a good teacher. He was. According to many of today's educators, Jesus was a masterful teacher. He led his audience through a verbal journey, using questions to make statements. Jesus' model of teaching was brilliant: ask questions and lead people to great understanding through simple storytelling.

Some skeptics claim that he was just a nice man. "Gentle" is how I describe him. Yet, in meekness, Jesus had the ability to be tough. He took on the Jewish rabbis and overturned their profit centers that had been set up in the lobby of the local church. The religious were using their platform to make a profit. It ticked him off, because he knew they were trying to turn profit off of pain. Yes, he was tender. He was also tough. I love how Dave Roberts described him in the book *Following Jesus*. He said that Jesus was a paradox.[2] His life was confusing and at times seemed a contradiction. How could Jesus have caused a revolution of belief and yet been so kind? How could he teach others to love their enemies, while he was being despised by his enemies?

Through the confusion, Jesus was defined clearly.

As I trekked through these thoughts, I saw that the Jesus I had been told about was not the Jesus of scripture. This man was so much about relationship. I'd been told he was all about rules.

If I missed it on this huge factor, maybe others had too.

Jesus modeled a life of love. Beyond teacher, rabbi, carpenter, and/or mystic, Jesus proclaimed a radical message of hope and love that was his singular cause of death. The religious order was irate that he emerged as a leader to common people.

Jesus understood that we are all broken and filled with missed moments in life that create great guilt. In an attempt to free humanity from rules and regulations, Jesus ticked religious people off. He neutralized the hold of their clenched fist of power.

He spoke of love.

He offered hope.

He gave affirmation and understanding.

He created community.

He spoke of and demanded an absolute inclusion of love for people with issues and doubts.

This message of inclusion went far beyond the claim of any other world religious leader in that he said he had the ability to make right what was wrong. He had the power to bring unfailing love to a confused and skeptical humanity.

Many people have not heard or read any of the statements that Jesus truly made. I am amazed when I talk to skeptics how many have not truly investigated his claims. I've asked those who doubt Jesus where their issue lands, and so many times it's not with him at all. It has been with rules that have replaced relationship. The issue has been with interpretation of scripture, not the investigation of a Savior.

For the skeptic who is tired, Jesus said, *"Come to me if you are tired, I will give you rest."*

For the skeptic who has been judged by the religious, Jesus said, *"I do not condemn you, nor does my Father who is in heaven."*

In an attempt to free humanity from rules and regulations, Jesus ticked religious people off. He neutralized the hold of their clenched fist of power.

For the skeptic who has been alone and lost in their over-analyzed thoughts, Jesus said, *"I am the way."*

For the skeptic who has been ripped off, lied to, and taken advantage of, Jesus said, *"I am the truth."*

For the skeptic who has believed Jesus was a narcissistic tyrant, he said, *"I came to serve you."*[3]

It is amazing that a man with this message could be so misrepresented and misunderstood.

My skeptic friends explain that their skepticism comes from a pursuit of a deeper, more analytical truth. When I dig deeper, it seems to me that it is a way to avoid getting burnt by a lie. From personal experience, I know that brokenness creates a protective mindset that would not, or could not, trust anyone.

Somewhere, maybe they had been burnt or had a promise broken. I can empathize with that. Even as a Christian, I am skeptical. Not of Jesus, just of people. After all, many who I had trusted had ultimately betrayed me. Or at least I thought they had. Amazing how much of life's issues come back to me and my responses.

Brokenness and betrayal—they are a deadly mix. Their effects had taken their toll in my life as a skeptic. Desperate and having realized I was detached from the very people that brought me life, I had to make a change. Committed to the man, and considering the message, I chose to investigate the method that made Jesus so controversial. What I discovered altered my life.

I was given a Bible and no instruction. A friend gave it to me with good intentions but no direction on where to start or what to read. For me, it centered on Jesus—not on a church, not on a religion, not on a set of social rules that maintained dogma . . . all things that were not at all central to Jesus.

I knew a little. I knew that his biography started in the second half, or the New Testament part, of the Bible. The first four books of the New Testament told the stories of who Jesus was to society and how he lived.

The stories had a central message, focused on communicating that singular truth: "Jesus loves you." But I began to put my broken puzzle pieces together as I uncovered *how* Jesus lived.

Jesus met people where they were in life. Scoffing and filled with cynicism, the religious called him "a friend to sinners."[4] They found him guilty on charges of loving people. I am amazed by the fact that he was embraced by the nonreligious and hated by the religious.

Those who didn't go to church loved him. He met their needs.

Those who were in the church hated him. He exposed their needs.

In the name of love, he lived.

This message of hope was preceded with acts of kindness. His willingness to meet a practical need before he asserted a spiritual answer proved that he cared about people where they were in life.

History books confirm the scriptural snapshot of Jesus' death. Hanging in between two criminals, he solidified our significance through his final acts of inclusion. This clearly changed the way I viewed life.

Jesus is the centerpiece of a decision each person must consider. This decision finds a metaphor in the three crosses that stood on that fateful Calvary hill where Jesus was crucified. As the three men hung there suffering to death, on the one side was a crook who blew Jesus off: "*If you are* the Son of God, come down from that cross and save us." On that side, a skeptic, imprisoned with nails and demanding proof.

On the other side, a simple request from a man who was guilty of a crime, broken, and about to die: "Remember me when you get to heaven." Jesus looked beyond all this second man's baggage and broken past and said, "Today you will *be with me* in paradise" (see Luke 23:39–43).

Society demands justice; Jesus delivered mercy. People want to get; Jesus gave. People want to forget; Jesus remembered. Skeptics demand an explanation; Jesus died to deliver the definition.

A pastor I heard communicated an interesting angle on Jesus and how he died. He reframed this dying thief's request. The speaker honed in on the simple request, "Will you remember me?" He supposed that perhaps there was more to the request of remembrance.

Re-membered. Was the crook asking for Jesus to have a fond recollection of him in heaven? Or, where the circumstance of life had dismembered him, was he asking the carpenter to *re-member* him? Was he asking to be put back together?[5]

"Hey, Jesus, I am broken. I have been betrayed. Can you re-member me? Can you put me back together?"

What has been eating at you?

What has left you empty?

What situation have you experienced that left you cynical and skeptical?

Who shattered your trust?

What has stolen your right to love and be loved?

Look into the scriptures and read how Jesus loved and listened unconditionally. You may need to ask Jesus to put you back together.

1. See John 15:9, 12.

2. Dave Roberts, *Following Jesus: A Non-Religious Guide for the Spiritually Hungry* (Lake Mary, FL: Relevant, 2004), 15–18.

3. See Matthew 11:28; Mark 10:45; John 8:11; 14:6.

4. See Luke 7:34.

5. Clint Brown, "Remember Me," *Alone* (Orlando, FL: Tribe, 2003), track 6.

Craig

My eyes stung from lack of sleep. It was hard even to focus on the Qantas Airline logo at the bottom right corner of the digital map. I dreaded the fourteen-hour flight from Australia back to the States.

There is something about airplane flights that gets my kids, Nolan and Elise, riled up. We've been on a midnight flight that you would have thought was at noon judging from their energy level. Of course for my wife, Jeanette, it had already been a long week. Because I was busy getting ready for the trip and communicating to everyone involved, the packing had fallen on her. She took care of the kids and made sure everything was packed. From granola to Sponge Bob to all the clothes, she packed it. And after ten days Down Under, I too was ready for home. My soul was tired, but I was leaving with some really good memories.

It was my second trip to Australia, and I love the place. The people have a genuine and good-natured approach to life—especially Steve, Ben, and Andy. It's odd that people are so kind, knowing the origin of this island's population. You see, Australia was a human dumping ground for broken and angry parts of humanity. Years ago, crooks, killers, thieves—

all prisoners—were taken from parts of Europe. They were dumped and left to die. But those same people created the first colonies of Australia, and from an ancestry of the incarcerated, a nation was established.

Redemption.

I reclined my seat back and reflected on the trip, amazed at how it even came about. But more importantly, I was amazed at what I had learned about Jesus, his creation, and his redemptive plan. Australia painted a stunning backdrop for Jesus' perspective and the value he places on his people. Despite people's bad decisions and derailed destinies, despite the overdose of self and the sabotage of self-discipline and daily structure, Jesus loves us anyway.

Despite people's bad decisions and derailed destinies, Jesus loves us anyway.

That's why we came here. After my first trip here, I learned of a youth pastor who stuck his face in the middle of the hedonistic hotels that housed an annual weeklong party called Schoolies. His efforts moved me, and I came as his friend to help him with the ruckus.

Getting Schooled

Located off the Gold Coast of Australia, the Schoolies party is an annual rite of passage where graduating high school students revel in all kinds of unhealthy craziness at the completion of their academic year. Think "Girls Gone Wild" on amphetamines. The recent graduates are ready to party with drunken all-nighters. For most of the students, this is the first time they experience a holiday without their family.

Don't misunderstand me: there are elements of the original concept that are fine, like sporting events, games, dances, new friends, and the like. But when gluttony showed up, the Schoolies got schooled.

Let me explain.

When Schoolies roll into town, hotel operators reserve their entire hotel for the partying students, who then take advantage of very little supervision to move toward their supposed adulthood. For many teens, gluttony is the goal: "get as much as you want as often as you want for as long as you want." But it equates to being too much, too soon, for too many. As usual, alcohol is the catalyst.

In Australia, it is illegal to buy, drink, or possess alcohol if you're under eighteen and in public view. Yet, drinking or possessing alcohol in private is legal, as long as it is purchased by an adult. This translates to "Get drunk. Just do it out of sight!"

The end of November is Schoolies Season, and this year was no different. Thousands gathered on the Gold Coast. Teens from all across Australia piled into airplanes and cars and made their way to the festivals. They were looking for a party, and I was there for it.

Looking back, I was stunned at what I saw as students carried their luggage to their rooms. Some suitcases were for clothes, others were filled with gallons of liquor. Scantily clad girls paraded in the hotel lobby. Guys with fresh tattoos, most likely inked specifically for this event, walked around shirtless, flexing. And the part that blew me away?

Many parents unloaded the alcohol they purchased for their kids and then kissed them goodbye.

My mind flashed back to when I was growing up. Some friends of mine called it "Lake Days." They would head to the lake in the early morning sun. Some would drink a few beers, but by late afternoon, it was over. Having to go home caused many to limit their consumption. At Schoolies, everything was different. Some stayed in their room nearly the whole time. Their time at Schoolies defined everything excessive, everything sensual, and everything hedonistic.

Some may think, "Kids will be kids." Or maybe "Out of sight, out of mind." But that's wrong. Without supervision to set some basic human parameters, many teens unknowingly gamble away aspects of their future by allowing gluttony to reign. Character, moral ethics, sobriety, purity, and respect for others get drowned in a giant pool of alcohol.

Gluttony was the game, and nearly everyone had come to play ball.

Simply put, gluttony is overindulgence. And to add another dimension to it, listen to what contemporary author Peter DeVries said: "Gluttony is an emotional escape, it is a sign something is eating us."[1] If DeVries was right, there is a root cause to overindulgence. I sat looking around the hotel lobby, and many Schoolies were already stumbling over their steps, intoxicated. *What could be eating at all these students?* I wondered. I tried to find an adult, other than myself. I couldn't. Even the hotel staff were in their early twenties.

Sitting near the elevator, I noticed a young, brown-haired

Gluttony was the game, and nearly everyone had come to play ball.

girl, maybe eighteen years old, who had obviously been drinking. She caught my eye because sleeping next to me was another brown-haired girl, my daughter, Elise. In just shy of two decades, I realized, Elise would be the same age as this girl. Her white shorts rode low on her hips, and it was obvious that she wanted the guys at Schoolies to look, lust, and lie in wait.

Many at Schoolies had already been hooked by the bait she had laid out for them. The neon bright color of her bathing suit bottom strings made two symmetric bows atop each hip. Her top was a bikini bra. Her tanned skin contrasted with her white shorts. She moved side to side as if a melody played in her head. It was a slow song. The rhythmic motion made my stomach sink. The guys who slowly began to move toward her saw a dancer. I saw some-one's daughter.

She hadn't been at Schoolies for more than a few hours, and her binge was already blinding her. The grim reaper called Gluttony was already claiming victims. The elevator door opened. Three guys got off the elevator. Two were zipping up their pants, and the third was giggling while he quickly tried to rewind what he had just captured on his digital video camera. They walked past the dancer in white, oblivious to her. They had already made their kill.

Another girl stumbled off behind the three of them. Her hair was matted. She tried to smile. I nearly cried. Within minutes, the three guys and the girl sat on a bench in the lobby together, all of them laughing at the video. She won't be laughing, I thought, when she sobers up and sees it on YouTube.

But the dancer still swayed. By now, guys cheered and yelped, pushing her to go further. I counted six or so of them hollering at her. They chanted. They wanted to conquer. As I watched their response to her every move, I realized none of them looked at life with the sense that there had to be more than this. Fearing the impression this scene would make on my daughter, I picked her up (still sleeping, thank God), and left.

Speaker Louie Giglio talks about it like this: In the hands of the Creator, we're paintbrushes with brilliant colors and hues. Each of these young people is a color, representing a valued trait of their destiny. But by breaching the human ethics that preserve the value of others, those brushes have been pried from God's hand. He had painted a masterpiece created before the beginning of time, a picture that represented their destiny, but debauchery, decadence, and derailment has no place in God's design.

With the brushes hijacked by each one of us who has ever pursued our own desires over God's, we have blotched, splattered, and smeared self into the painting. The canvas of our character has been compromised.

> In the hands of the Creator, we're paintbrushes with brilliant colors and hues.

The primary color of self-indulgence is the hue of gluttony.

Stepping out of the lobby, I noticed a kid sitting on the side of the parking lot. His face looked white and pale. In between his legs was bile and vomit. Gluttony gripped him too.

Nearly everyone, hijacked. Nearly everywhere.

Red Frog Redemption

In 1997, my friend Andy Gourley saw what was going on during Schoolies Week. As a youth pastor, he was crushed to see so much pain in so many young people. While on vacation, Andy visited one of his friends at Schoolies Week and was overwhelmed at the need for young people to be kept safe as they celebrated. He knew that the only way to reach the students was by serving them.

Armed only with some bags of Red Frog Candy (an Australian candy similar to Gummi Worms but oh so much better), Andy broke the ice and found ways to meet the needs of the students. The following year, he gave out more Red Frogs. Hotel lobbies became a place to meet kids where they were. Andy recruited friends to multiply his efforts, and the Red Frog Chaplaincy Network was created.

At Schoolies Week celebrations, Red Frogs Australia has four main roles: visitation, referral, mediation, and diversionary activities. The Red Frog Crew, made up of over 600 volunteers, aims to support Schoolies through their weeklong celebrations and provide a positive presence amongst their partying culture. They also assist Schoolies by walking young people home, cooking pancakes, cleaning rooms, handing out Red Frogs, and offering emotional support through what can often be a challenging week.

Red Frogs Entertainment is the best of its kind, and Schoolies love the craze of the Red Frog Stage at locations on the Gold Coast and Airlie Beach.

Red Frogs is doing great work. In one incident a couple years back, two Red Frog chaplains physically restrained a teen from jumping to his death. They've stopped fights, carried drunks home, and derailed assaults of every kind. The Red Frogs are committed to serving gluttons with grace.

That's why I was in Australia. I got to stand before the leaders, chaplains, volunteers, pastors, and donors who made Red Frogs a success. I told them that they were doing what Jesus would be doing. He would be in the bars and clubs, the hotels and beaches. He would clean the puke and carry the passed-out partier. He would pray. He would persuade with his actions and encourage with his words. It's true: Jesus loves gluttons. Even better than speaking to the Red Frogs one night at their service was joining them in action.

My first night there I grabbed a bag of the Red Frogs candies and headed out with a team of people. Five different Schoolies said to me that night, "Next year I want to be a Red Frog." That made my night. Those five people assured me that this team of six hundred-plus volunteers was making an impact. We headed from the dance party that was taking place on the beach toward the hotel rooms. We split up into smaller groups and just started knocking on hotel doors. Never was a door shut in our face or a door not opened or were we refused entry. In the midst of a bunch of Schoolies partying in their rooms, we were invited in for conversation. We made pancakes, we walked kids home, we were on the scene for a few suicide attempts and stood in the call center to hear confessions of a rape and other crimes.

> **Five different Schoolies said to me that night, "Next year I want to be a Red Frog."**

Red Frogs were always first on the scene. No matter if it was cleaning up puke in the hotel room, picking kids up out of the elevators and carrying them back to their rooms, walking kids back to their hotels, or just sitting in their hotel rooms. The Red Frogs cared for these Schoolies.

The first time I met Andy and learned of Schoolies, he said, "In order to win this generation, you must serve this generation." Thousands of volunteers, a $500,000 annual budget, and seven tons of Red Frogs is what his outreach looks like each year. He is welcomed by the hotel staff, the students, and everyone in sight. He's been given free hotel rooms and has now expanded his outreach to college campus parties across Australia. In fact, Red Frogs has a presence at over 180 universities worldwide.

Everything about Schoolies told you that more is better. The more sex you could have, the more alcohol you could drink. Red Frogs' motto was just the opposite. Over and over I kept hearing from the organizers of the Frogs, "Find your one." Find your one person you made a connection with and key in on that. Go back to that hotel room, follow up with that one person. It reminded me about the parable where Jesus talks about the shepherd who leaves his flock to go after the one lost sheep. Sometimes more is not better.

Sunday night I was exhausted. After finishing a week at Schoolies and two church services in the morning over in Brisbane about an hour from where Schoolies was held, I had one more church service to speak at. This was the young adults service over at Citipointe church. I got to mix it up a bit and did not do the standard porn talk I often get asked to preach. I talked about Schoolies. I talked about the Frogs. I talked about how Jesus came for the sick, not the healthy. The gluttons. A few hands went up that night during the invitation to accept the love of Jesus. In the lobby afterward, I met three Red Frogs. They looked even more exhausted than me. After a week of service at Schoolies, they were back in their city and at church. There were not just three of them in their group. There were six. You see, each of them had found their one. A smile spread across my face so large when I heard that the three Schoolies who these Frogs had poured into the whole week decided to come to church. I recognized one of the Schoolies, because just a few minutes earlier I saw his hand in the air during the invitation. His life was changed because someone gave up their week to serve him, and he found out about Someone who lost his life so that he might have life.

I live in Vegas, the gluttony capital of the world. The sensuous stripper ads that line the Strip advertise gluttony. One ad said, "More Women. More Lust. More of Everything. Vegas!" That's why I live here: to communicate to every person that Jesus loves the glutton. We have come to Vegas to *be* the church, not necessarily to start one. We call our ministry The Strip Church and have centered it around the Las Vegas Strip. But you don't have to come to Vegas to find gluttony. Go to a sports bar on a Friday night. Go to an all-you-can-eat buffet on Sunday morning. Talk with your local police about whether prostitution is a problem in your town.

Gluttony is everywhere. And yet, when was the last time you heard a sermon or presentation about it? I think I've heard it once in my whole life.

But it's really not the focus. The focus is that people are committed to consumption. And consumption to mass levels fills voids, but only temporarily.

Think of a guy who is morbidly obese. Do you think that as a child he dreamed of the day he would grow up and become grotesquely unhealthy? Of course not. Somewhere along the way, he came to believe eating fills a void. The more overeaters consume, the more they assume the void is being filled.

Think of the woman who is an alcoholic. Do you think one day she said, "I want to kill myself through a slow infection in my liver caused by alcohol?" Of course not. Unhealthy as it may be, alcohol fills a void, temporarily. It convinces the mind that reality is suspended. The alcoholic is convinced that the void is covered. But it is only when the buzz is kept. Lose the buzz and the pain returns. With each sip, the next buzz is more fleeting.

In the late 1980s, Guns N' Roses lead singer Axl Rose summed up gluttony. I remember when the tape cassette came out, and we belted out these songs during freshman gym class: "I used to do a little, but a little won't do it. So a little got more and more."[2]

That's gluttony: seeking more and more to fill the voids of life.

When Jesus stepped onto the scene, he wanted to fill the void. The weight of every pain, the depth of every void, was consumed by his willingness to abide with us. When we realize that Jesus purposed us to live life at its best, it doesn't include indulgence of harmful things. The scriptures describe this cryptic encounter with Christ. In Revelation 3:20, the encounter paints a clearly metaphoric picture of his willingness to dwell within: "Behold, I stand at the door and knock. If anyone hears My voice and opens the door, I will come in to him" (NKJV).

He fills the void. No longer is "more, more, more" the mantra. The glutton can find wholeness in Christ. The New Testament writer Paul described it this way: "So that Christ may dwell in your hearts through faith."[3]

For the one who has overconsumed, let Jesus calm you.

For the one who gorges on food, indulge on the Bread of Life. It will fulfill you.

For the one who drowns their sorrows in a liquid counselor, there is Living Water. It will quench.

And for all of us who see the damage of gluttony in our friends or in our family, keep bringing Jesus to them.

This I know: Jesus loves the glutton.

---

1. Peter DeVries (1910–1993), American editor and novelist.
2. Guns N' Roses, "Mr. Brownstone," *Appetite for Destruction* (Geffen Records, 1987).
3. Ephesians 3:17.

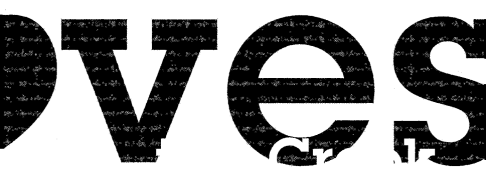

Jason

His face lit up the church lobby before worship began. Smiling ear to ear, the gentleman placed his left hand on the small of his wife's back as they stood side by side speaking to another couple. His right hand gripped a Bible that had obviously been read. I knew this guy. Noticing his attire, I assumed we had met in the corporate world, where I speak occasionally to large groups. His tan dress pants were wrinkle-free and pressed to perfection. His shirt was a long-sleeve, button-up polo, stiff from extra starch. It too was wrinkle-free, tucked in with a brown leather belt securing its placement. I recognized the shoes. I had told my wife only days earlier that I wanted a pair of those. Everything on this guy was impressive.

As he placed his order for his coffee, his natural baritone voice gave him away. I had not seen him in more than twenty years, but I knew that voice anywhere.

It was "Edward." His friends called him Eddie.[1]

Memories flooded my mind. The last time I saw Eddie was when we were ninth graders, and he had that deep voice even then. I met him through a couple mutual friends, but otherwise we did not have much in common. I had been raised in the suburbs of Sacramento; he lived in the city. Our schools were different. Our clothes were different. Our lives were different.

By the time he was fourteen, Eddie was bitter over his parents' divorce, which happened when he was only six years old. Wanting acceptance and love, yet not seeing a solid male figure in his life, he lashed out. His anger was rooted in the fact that he had to be his mother's provider and could not do it. He did not know how.

Quickly, what began as petty crime escalated to full-on burglary. Drugs on the streets were easy to get. He found power in being able to bully. His petty crimes were exchanged for more sinister plots. Everything, including his drug use, was amplified. By sixteen he was shooting crank (methamphetamine) into his veins. It emboldened him. That same year, he started a riot at his high school and paid the crooked vice-principal off with dope.

The risk increased because of his crime sprees. His exposure to the California State prison system was inevitable. Eddie had carved out a young life defined by criminal activity. Despite a faithful mom who prayed and always taught him the way of Jesus, his world continued to spin out of control.

The first stint of hard time for Eddie was his eight-year sentence to the notorious Folsom State Prison (FSP). Known for its violence and rough conditions, FSP has housed some notable inmates. From Sonny Barger of the Hell's Angels to Suge Knight, owner of Death Row Records, and even Charles Manson, it is not a county jail setup. It is a place designed to control violent criminals: rapists, murderers, extortionists, thieves, and a young man who had lost his way in the wilderness of bitterness and brokenness. Eddie.

When the gates of FSP opened, the thought was to do good solid time and eradicate his eight-year sentence as quickly as possible. Walking the tier for the first time, he heard the hollers and verbal assaults meant to scare the "new arrivals." This was prison, and there was a new set of rules. (Note: Edward's specific crimes and affiliations cannot be identified for his safety and that of others.)

Life became a game of survival on the inside. He knew the more violence he was willing to volunteer for, the more respect others would give him. He could make a name for himself. The prison guards knew him as a number. The gang new him as "Short E."

God knew him as "Son."

Eddie was as violent as ever—so violent that he spent most of his time in "The Hole," an isolated cell intended to punish inmates who couldn't play by the rules. He sat daily in this classroom of silence. In lockdown, Eddie was living out his life as a prisoner, identified only by a number. His existence was without purpose. Inevitably, as soon as he was released from isolation, erratic behavior usually sent him back.

The criminally minded crook was paroled again and again. After eight times of getting out and going back, something had to change. Corcoran, Soledad, Solano, and New Folsom are the places he was sentenced to for more crimes. Mostly crimes he committed while in prison. This got Eddie more time in isolation. The power struggle and constant anxiety of having to look over his shoulder wore on him.

The stories of murder, extortion, rape, drugs, and violence behind the prison walls would exhaust anyone. The praying momma who melted the exterior hardness of Eddie painted a clear picture that Jesus had the ability to take away the pain, the problems, and the pent-up aggression in his angry heart. But as with any gang, especially those thriving behind prison walls, there would be a price to pay for this career criminal.

Three Crooks' Crosses

Criminals were prosecuted to the fullest extent of the law in the first-century Roman courts of Caesar. Jesus had been captured and tried in what was a court in name only. More of a hostile court of public opinion, people who once revered Jesus had flipped on him. Days before, when Jesus entered into Jerusalem, many faithful followers had waved palm branches at him. Palm leaves were a symbol of the Maccabean revolt when Jews had overthrown the rule of the Antiochus leadership years earlier. The branches were a symbol of this revolt and banners of rebels. The crowd thought Jesus was going to lead another revolt. They were ready to rebel. And they did.

Days later, they rebelled against the one who came to save the world.

They rebelled against the one who came to save the world.

Days earlier, they loved. On this day, they loathed and chanted, "Crucify him." The religious of the day were incensed at the audacity of this man who claimed to be God. Their hatred filled the air as a maddened mob demanded death.

A cruel crowd looked up at the steep hill on the outskirts of Jerusalem, the staging site of execution for all criminals. The cross of Christ was one of three staked into the ground. Resembling a skull, the hill called Golgotha was where crooks and common criminals were left to die on a piece of cruel timber. It was morbid in nature. Golgotha and its garbage heap surroundings made the place of Jesus' death a humiliating place to die.

Once found guilty, the criminal would be taken to a place of public spectacle. Many historical scholars believe that the original punishment given to Jesus was scourging, which would have been bad enough. But the scripture's assessment of the maddened mob provoked an additional sentence to satisfy their hatred and lust for blood. Those in opposition to Jesus—the religious—despised his shameless claim of deity. They thought of him as a common criminal, a crook who deserved to be murdered for having the audacity to love the unloved.

The Roman soldier began the beating, using a *flagrum*. This tool of torture was a short whip laced with many long, leather straps that had two small balls of lead attached at the ends. As it snapped in its recoil, it would rip through flesh. The heavy whip was slammed with full force across Jesus' shoulders, back, and legs.

I'm not sure what I would have felt had I been there in the crowd. Would I have shouted "crucify him" or "have compassion on him"? How would you have responded? Those standing there must have felt like you and I feel when we have seen a brutal car accident. It's horrific, but we still drive by slowly, looking to catch a glance. I liken the crucifixion to a spiritual snuff film.

With each blow, deeper into the tissues, blood oozed. Capillaries, veins, layers of skin, and then the bleeding from beneath the muscle must have caused a sense of shock to all who watched. Which was worse—the pain in the body or the sting of the skeptics?

Historians write, "The severe scourging, with its intense pain and appreciable blood loss, most probably left Jesus in a pre-shock state. His skin was shredded. The physical and mental abuse meted out by the Jews and the Romans, as well as the lack of food, water and sleep, also contributed to his generally weakened state. Therefore, even before the actual crucifixion, Jesus' physical condition was at least serious and possibly critical."[2] Should they survive the scourge, most crooks wished for death.

Jesus was slapped with a piece of wood across his back. The horizontal timber dug into his torn flesh. Preexisting pain made the weight of the heavy wood agonizing. Compared to what he had already endured, the pain from the crossbar splinters would have barely registered on this Richter scale of torture.

The Christ who the Roman government called a crook joined two criminals. There on Golgotha, Jesus hung on a wooden image of redemption that salvaged mankind and sealed them unto God.

> For the Son of Man came to seek and to save what was lost.
>
> Luke 19:10

But so many choose to ignore the claims of Jesus, negate the cross, because most don't think of themselves as a crook.

Some skeptics assert that the claims of Jesus' life and death are supported solely by Christians. Some, who are unaware of the heaps of historical fact, have gone as far as to say Jesus never existed. Never existed?

Secular historians who never followed Jesus have affirmed the historical value and validity of Jesus and his demise. Josephus, a historian alive at the time of Jesus, was one of the most concise in his accounts:

> Now, there was about this time Jesus, a wise man . . . he was a doer of wonderful works—a teacher of such men as receive the truth with pleasure. He drew over to him both many of the Jews, and many of the Gentiles. . . . When Pilate, at the suggestion of the principal men amongst us, had condemned him to the cross, those that loved him at the first did not forsake him and the tribe of Christians, so named from him, are not extinct at this day.[3]

History shows that the Roman government crucified Jesus. Many Jewish people did not believe that Jesus was the Messiah. Yet even their Talmud affirms Jesus' existence:

> On the eve of the Passover Yeshu [Jesus] was hanged [crucified]. For forty days before the execution took place, a herald went forth and cried, "He is going forth to be stoned because he has practiced sorcery and enticed Israel to apostasy. Any one who can say anything in his favor, let him come forward and plead on his behalf." But since nothing was brought forward in his favor he was hanged on the eve of the Passover![4]

Jesus hung between two crooks who were nailed to a cross to pay for their crimes. It was a scene of doubt. It was a scene of destiny. From the framework of my own life, I see pieces of myself in both crooks.

On one side, there was a hardened crook, rebellious even unto death. Maybe he believed he had gone too far and the claims of Jesus were beyond his reach. Maybe he just didn't want to submit to a cause bigger than himself. When Jesus was hoisted up, the pride within this prisoner caused him to mock and question the deity of God in Jesus. In the middle of his pain, he was still angry at life. With gritted teeth, seething in hatred, self-reliance, and ego, he refused to accept the Hope for all eternity.

Then there was the other crook. He hung in suspended humility. Broken and lost, dejected and desperate, he made a final appeal. Most likely near suffocation from collapsed lungs, the crook cried out. His bellow was a request of remembrance: "Jesus, remember me."

From the framework of my own life, I see pieces of myself in both crooks.

"Today, you will be with me in paradise," Jesus responded. A life of crime was blotted out by instantaneous forgiveness. No checklist of commitments. No church attendance. No tithing. No baptism, even. While those things are important, they are ultimately peripheral. Jesus wants crooks to be connected, even if only for the length of a last dying breath.

Jesus wants reconciliation. He wants a relationship.

Despite our moral compasses, every person has criminal tendencies. Call it the crook within. Scripture describes how each person has failed and continuously fallen short of God's perfect plan. When we miss in one area of conscience or conviction, we miss in all areas. Here is what the New Testa-

> **Jesus wants reconciliation. He wants a relationship.**

ment says: when you have broken one command, you have broken them all.[5]

But Jesus can rescue us. In his book *The Gutter*, Craig wrote:

Because of missing the mark, man and God are separated. Because of the mistakes we make (i.e., sin) we are separated from the holy and perfect God. But we don't have to stay that way, according to the next stepping stone, Romans 5:8: "But God demonstrates his own love for us in this: While we were still sinners, Christ died for us." While we were still missing the mark, in the middle of our mess, God expressed His desire to be reunited to us, a desire that took human form in the man of Jesus. In a sense, Jesus went to the gutter specifically to get us out of it. He even said so Himself when He told the disciples nobody could ever get to God, escaping the gutter, unless they go through Him (John 14:6). After all, Jesus is the only one who ever conquered it.

Paul must have been addressing the book of Romans to a bunch of skeptics, because he fires off the reason why sins and mistakes must be accounted for in chapter 6, verse 23: "For the wages of sin is death, but the gift of God is eternal life in Christ Jesus our Lord." The results of a life in sin: Death. Yes, death! The sure way to die is to live in the gutter, in total separation from God. Many say, "Come on, a physical death? Please!" But I'm more concerned about a spiritual death than a physical death, since Jesus told us not to worry about what will happen to our physical body, but to take care of our spiritual lives first (Matt. 6:25–34).

When Jesus hung on the cross, He did so desiring that every person would accept His free gift of life. The only qualifier is that you believe in Him, and I'm not talking about a belief of existence here, either—even demons believe that. I'm talking about a belief in the values, standards, and purpose of confessing that Jesus Christ is who He said He is and will do what He said He would do. It's a belief that's so strong, you aren't afraid to articulate it, which is exactly what the next stepping stone calls for. Romans 10:9 says, that if "you confess with your mouth, 'Jesus is Lord,' and believe in your heart that God raised him from the dead, you will be saved." Four verses later, the Bible says the same thing: "Everyone who calls on the name of the Lord will be saved."[6]

Do you want fulfillment and freedom? Sometimes we just don't know how to get there. Sometimes we don't know how to explain the longing in the depths of our hearts. We don't know how to embrace it. Rules and regulations of religion have imprisoned so many of the faithful. The only thing that can abolish pain and unfulfilled purpose in life is a relationship with Jesus, who loves everyone, including the most crooked, vile criminal.

Changed Crook?

Had I known where Eddie had been for the last twenty years, I may not have approached him as confidently as I did. Sometimes those with dark paths have chosen to go to our church to blend in and worship in anonymity. They slip into a back row or balcony for a few months and then, once they are acquainted with the vibe, slowly acclimate. Had I known he had been locked up, I would have thought through the way I touched base.

"Is your name Eddie?" I asked.

Eddie looked at me, still blowing on his coffee to cool it. He tilted his head slightly to look over his eyeglasses and asked, "Do I know you?"

Had I known prison time was on his résumé, I would have understood the twinge of suspicion in his voice. I paused for a second and then threw it out there in my best minister's voice. "It's Jason Harper, from the old school."

Short E's smile slowly faded, and his next words carried a slight edge. "Which old school?"

My "Old School" and his "Old School" were two entirely different things. He later told me that he was often approached in public by old enemies from prison.

I quickly gave him the rundown of our common friends, our connections, and our crossed paths. Once again the smile that lit up the lobby returned to Eddie's face. We shared a brief introduction of our wives and shook hands, excited to have been reacquainted. He explained he had been coming to Capital Christian Center for church on Sundays for about a year and had not seen me, or at least had not put the two-decade-old separation puzzle together. As we parted, I asked, "What's been going on?"

He smiled. "Let's talk it over at lunch."

A few weeks later, our families gathered after church and I learned everything. And I mean *everything*. He told me how, after his eight parole violations, he was sent back to prison. His gang in prison had informed all its members that a riot was going to occur, and participation was not optional. The dilemma he faced was the knowledge that if he got nailed in the riot he would add months, if not years, onto his already painful return. With only a glimmer of knowledge of Jesus but a confidence in the truth of scripture, he decided to stand in his cell door and pray that he would not be sucked into a death sentence.

The echo of the iron doors opening on his cell block marked the beginning of the violent coup. For the first time in years, he whispered, "God, please don't let me die." Something profound happened. That whisper for intervention moved Eddie from being a hardened crook on one side of the cross to the other side, just as a criminal long ago had called out: "Today, remember me in paradise."

With a full-scale riot occurring, a once-evil conscience cajoled him to reconsider his decision to stay put. Imagine the thoughts in his head: "Short E, you have done this hundreds of times. Look at you cowering in this cage. Get out and fight!" But the taunting landed on deaf ears. With one cry for Christ, an entire outlook changed.

Minutes passed, but it seemed like hours. Eddie crouched, ducked, stood in his cell knowing that his aluminum bunk could not shield him; only God could. Rival gang members walked the cell block tier toward him. They were hunting for the vulnerable and the exposed. They wanted an easy kill. As they ran toward him, he stood, his fear mounting like he had never felt before. Thoughts of his praying mom, his stupid decisions that led him to this point, his wife, his kids, his home, and even thoughts of his childhood flooded his mind in an instant.

With a silent prayer that God would redirect his rivals, he choked out, "Don't kill me. Let it go. I am done."

With those words, "Short E" was silenced, and Edward looked at the men with a new vision of humanity. Corrupt as they were, these were two more crooks for whom Jesus died.

"I was shocked. They looked at me with a stare and turned the other way," Edward confessed. "I don't expect those who have not been in that predicament to fully understand the depth of that miracle. God saved me in that cell."

Within months, Edward paroled for the last time and was finally free.

Years removed, we sat with our families and ate lunch. I was puzzled and perplexed at the transformation that had occurred in his life. As we finished, Eddie answered the question that I had asked nearly two hours earlier when we first sat down, "What has God called you to do?"

"I want to be a pastor. I want to study the scriptures. I want to give my loyalty and allegiance to God with the same passion I did the gang." He was convinced.

Less than a week later, he enrolled in Bible college courses through Global University. As he's taken his perfectionist nature to the academic world, Eddie now frequently calls me to ask for clarity on scripture. Each day he is reminded of the love Jesus has for him.

> "I want to give my loyalty and allegiance to God with the same passion I did the gang."

A few months ago, Edward's family celebrated another year removed from prison. He had finished his parole. Those who love him gathered together, and he stood in front of his family and friends and spoke eloquently of God's intervention. He understands both sides of the cross. He understands the hardened. He understands the humbled. He understands the criminal, crooked-minded person who has broken one and therefore every measure of God's perspectives and parameters. He understands the need that he and I, you and yours, have for a Savior.

He understands that Jesus loves crooks.

1. To protect his identity, these are false names/nicknames.

2. W. D. Edwards., W. J. Gabel, and F. E. Homer, "On the Physical Death of Jesus Christ," *JAMA*, vol. 255, no. 11 (1986), 1455–63.

3. *The Antiquities of the Jews*, 18.63–64, in ibid. This text is widely thought to have been edited by early Christian influences; the shown quotation is generally accepted as the original text of Josephus.

4. Remarks added. From the reading in *The Babylonian Talmud*, trans. I. Epstein (1935), vol. III, Sanhedrin 43a, p. 281, as quoted in Gary R. Habermas, *The Historical Jesus: Ancient Evidence for the Life of Christ* (Joplin, MO: College Press Publishing Co., 1996), 203.

5. See James 2:10.

6. Craig Gross, *The Gutter: Where Life Is Meant to Be Lived* (Orlando, FL: Relevant Media Group, 2005), 93–94.

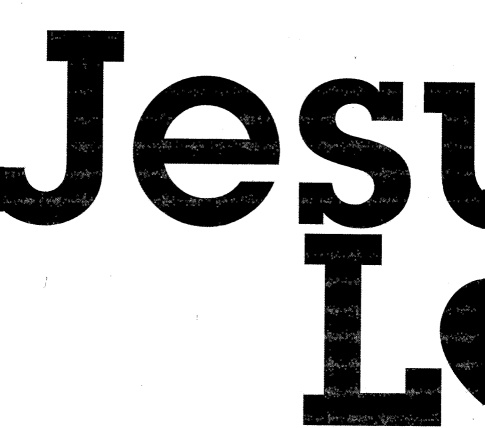

Jason

There is something about the downtown corridor of my city that I can't fully explain. It sits on the edge of a large river whose flowing water is held back by hundred-year-old levees. Oddly, Sacramento was listed as one of the most "at-risk" cities for flooding in the nation, second only to New Orleans, and we all know what happened there. We are still hoping *our* levees never break.

In some places, the city streets sit below the river's seasonal water level. But that doesn't stop a bustling, revitalized area that draws shoppers, tourists, street vendors, and even political enthusiasts who want to get a glimpse of California's state capital. Occasionally, people will see "The Governator" Arnold Schwarzenegger at the state capitol or at a nearby restaurant.

But that's not what I love about this area. Sitting in any one of the twenty coffee shops I frequent in downtown Sacramento, I am gripped by the diversity of people—different ethnicities, different stages of life, different socioeconomic statuses, different hopes and dreams. I like to think of myself as a culturist. I have friends from every thread of the vast cultural swatch that is Sacramento's fabric. I know people in nearly every field of work. I have friends who are wealthy and friends who are homeless. I like to be around people who are not like me. As I watch people walk by, I am reminded why *Time* called Sacramento the most diverse city in America. It makes life interesting, and it validates to some extent the faith I choose to believe—faith in a God who loves absolutely everybody.

I go downtown to write. Often I will slip out the back door and go into the city. With only about a fifteen-minute drive from my office, I can be parked and sipping a cup of coffee in less than thirty minutes. According to the 2000 US Census, over ninety languages are spoken in our small Northern California town of 1.6 million people.[1] America is made of immigrants, many who have arrived legally through naturalization. Others have arrived after long nights and hot days of walking across the desert to crawl through a hole in a barbed-wire fence called a border.

The reality is, for whatever reason, some people choose to hate other people for very shallow reasons, like skin color or sexual orientation. Others, like the street people who sleep on benches or push their grocery carts from dumpster to dumpster, are treated as if they do not exist. Some are alienated, some are ignored, and some are isolated.

Then there are the junkies, those addicted to one substance or another, who live constantly in the prison of their own compulsions. Outcasts. That's what we sometimes call them. People who have been "cast out" in one way or another from mainstream society. But no matter where they came from or how they got here, they are people Jesus died for.

Jesus loves outcasts.

> **No matter where they come from or how they got here, they are people Jesus died for.**

Today, as I sat down to write this chapter, I pulled into Peet's Coffee on the corner of 20th and J Street. It's a quaint place with great ambiance. It usually has its share of outcasts who linger near or in the establishment. And I find myself wondering what each person's story is. Where did they come from? What makes them act the way they do? What makes me act the way I do?

Lavender Heights Loved

Peet's sits on the edge of the loosely dubbed Lavender District, the epicenter of Sacramento's gay culture. Also called Lavender Heights, it's approximately a four-square-block area, with most of the businesses being gay-owned and catering to lesbian, gay, bisexual, and transgender (LGBT) clientele. The gay/lesbian bars and clubs proclaim their friendly and inclusive environment to the surrounding community. The willow-tree-shaded streets are lined with many other places where LGBTs socialize. Many in Sacramento do not know the Lavender District exists; if they did, they would never set foot in it.

While standing in line to get a coffee, I noticed the woman in front of me. Her dark hair was pulled back into a tight ponytail, and she wore a tie-dyed ankle-length dress, with a macramé shoulder bag slung over her shoulder. I thought, *Wow, she's a throwback to the sixties*. But when she turned around, she had a full-length beard that rivaled ZZ Top.

"She" was actually a "he."

I wouldn't say I was shocked. I just remembered I was downtown, and downtown people believe and live differently than I do. Some people walked by him and offered a nonverbal snarl. To them, he was an outcast.

I see outcasts as those who have no boundaries and no borders. They have no social homeland. Outcasts are those who are the least among us. They are scorned, shunned, ostracized, and shelved. Maybe it is because of their ethnicity or national origin. Maybe it happens because of their actions or lack of social graces. Maybe it is because they're homeless and are seen as a blight on the cityscape. Regardless, they are outcasts.

But there is a whole other subculture who are also deemed outcasts, at least in the church. They are people with same-sex attractions or those in same-sex relationships. Many in the Christian community treat homosexuals as outcasts. I have seen firsthand how some of my gay friends have been verbally judged, to the point of being condemned for their lifestyle.

I am not confused about where I stand on this issue. I just find it odd that over the years the evangelical movement has

> **I have never seen picket signs and petitions protesting overeating or gossip or adultery.**

made this area a social punching bag, a pet sin to bash. It's quickly covered with a trifling quotation. "We don't hate the sinner, just the sin." I heard this once from a group of people who had just finished yelling condemnation and hurling out-of-context scriptures at a group of gay men who walked by.

I find it interesting and completely hypocritical that some yell the loudest about this area of culture, all the while ignoring other blatant cultural atrocities. Why pick on this sin as opposed to others? I have never seen picket signs and petitions protesting overeating or gossip or adultery.

Gay Joe

I remember the day I met Joe.

It was a beautiful afternoon as I officiated a wedding for two friends. They had chosen a downtown church that was built in the early 1900s, maybe earlier. The church had a venerable history and heritage. It was not far from the Lavender District.

I finished the wedding for the young couple. The groom had grown up in the youth group I had led, and the bride had graduated from the Christian school on our campus. Both lovebirds were excited the wedding celebration had gone well.

The wedding party exited the sanctuary, and I slowly followed. Oftentimes at weddings, I'm the last one to leave the building, and this day was no different. I walked off the platform and into Joe. The sixty-plus-year-old man was the church's wedding ceremony coordinator. He had short white hair and dressed well. He looked like he could have been the neighborhood postman for the Brady Bunch. He spoke softly and smiled, a much different demeanor than when he had to make sure the wedding party of feisty twenty-somethings paid attention. He conducted the wedding instructions so confidently. With only a little interaction and even less friendship equity, I simply said "thank you" as I exited the church.

Joe thanked me for the kind words of blessing during the wedding and then asked *The Question*. I say *The Question* because I had never been asked it before.

"What is it like doing a wedding in a church that is so open, affirming, and loving?"

It was packaged as an innocent inquiry, but there was more to it. Joe knew that I worked at Capital Christian Center, and he was implying two things. First, that I was not used to an "open, affirming, and loving" environment; second, that Capital was not like *this* church.

"I love doing weddings at Capital; it's a great and loving place!" This was my way of reversing his intended direction, and it perplexed him.

"You mean Capital is *open* and *accepting*?" he asked.

Wanting to talk more but needing to get to the exiting bride and groom, I said "Joe, let's get coffee soon." I was surprised when he accepted my invitation by handing me his business card with his cell and home number penned on the back. I hoped we could connect for coffee. I wanted to speak love and life into him.

I desperately wanted to explain, "It's not what you think," about my church. I wondered what created Joe's perception. Was it some angry do-gooder who said "God doesn't love queers and fags!" Maybe it was a myth built by that angry preacher I saw yelling on TBN that homosexual people were going to hell. That same preacher stood ever so portly, pointing his preaching finger at the camera: "Sodomites, gays, lesbians, and their anti-Christ perversion will spend eternity in a place where the worm dieth not." He even added some King James to his quote. He was sweating profusely and dabbed his forehead with his favorite preaching hanky. He must have been pushing three hundred pounds. Yet he never added to the list in his rant the deadly sin of gluttony. Gorging gets a free pass.

Who knows? Maybe it was me who gave Joe the feeling that he was an outcast in a church. I have made some stupid comments in the name of righteousness.

Not long after that day, I gave Joe a call to meet for coffee. As he sat across from me, he was stunned that we had established a friendship. He mattered to me, but more than that, he was a person whose fate was paid in full by the God I serve. Unfortunately, he had not always felt like he mattered to those who spoke for God.

Joe was a former board member of the Lambda Movement in Sacramento and, at one point, the vice president of the Lambda Center. As he explained its history, I learned the source of Joe's general perception of Christians. And I was horrified at what I later confirmed was the source of Lambda's start-up money.

> Jerry Falwell was forced to pay gay activist Jerry Sloan $5,000 after losing a court battle. During a TV debate in Sacramento, Falwell falsely denied calling the gay-oriented Metropolitan Community Churches "brute beasts" and "a vile and Satanic system" that will "one day be utterly annihilated and there will be a celebration in heaven." When Sloan insisted he had a tape, Falwell promised $5,000 if he could produce it. Sloan did, Falwell refused to pay, and Sloan successfully sued. Falwell appealed, with his

attorney alleging that the Jewish judge in the case was prejudiced. Falwell lost again and was forced to pay an additional $2,875 in sanctions and court fees.[2]

If I understood him correctly, Joe had a front row seat to this insanity. I had to take a moment to recover from my own pain about all this.

I told Joe that one of our core values at Capital Christian Center was to create an atmosphere of acceptance. I explained that we wanted our attenders to live a life of irresistible influence. Joe was hooked on the message of inclusive love.

I apologized to Joe. Over a cup of coffee, he had come face-to-face with a representative of the mythical right-winged monster that had been, proverbially speaking, chasing him for years. He didn't expect me to be the face of the monster called "an evangelical." I only wanted to show him God's love through an authentic friendship. The church he thought hated him loved him. It welcomed him in to grow and to discover more of God. God loves and accepts people where they are, not where we think they should be.

Failing to see the blindness caused by my own ignorance, I have made some bigoted remarks and packaged it as holiness. I failed to see that ignorance, hatred, and judgment for a fellow man is equally, if not more, distasteful to the love of a Romans 5:8 God. Here is my paraphrase of that scripture: "God loved me, you, the outcast, so much, that even while I was still making horrible deci-

> **God loves and accepts people where they are, not where we think they should be.**

sions, he sent Jesus, the full expression of his love, to die on the cross for me."

Joe and I met for coffee many times and kept developing trust, despite disagreements on certain things. With every disagreement, civility remained the conversational anchor. I started telling many of my friends about the impact Joe's conversations were having on my empathy.

I have another friend named Joe, so to clarify the two, I started referring to the one as Gay Joe. The first time I accidentally called him Gay Joe in front of him, he smiled and said, "I *am* gay and my name *is* Joe." It was his way of saying he wasn't upset with me classifying which Joe he was to my other friends.

Joe was in a twenty-year relationship with his partner, Ray, and just the other day he asked if my wife and I would double date with them. I told him yes, and later on that month, my wife and I hit the town with them. With no agenda, the dinner conversation quickly turned to a Q&A on why I do what I do. I spoke deeply about my belief in Jesus and his love for every person.

Critics asked why I would go to dinner with these people. Because that is where Jesus would be found spending time. He would be hosting a party or a dinner where others could come to learn about his unconditional love.

If you disagree, I understand. Perhaps you learned a sectarian form of thinking. Maybe you bought the lie that these "self-made outcasts" chose to be shunned, as if they wanted to be hated and judged. You bought a lie that their sin is an abomination and therefore should be looked on as worse than the next person's. The reality is, there are other Old

Testament abominations: wearing leather products, paying interest, and eating lobster.

I apologized to Joe for the pain he has felt from those within the faith community. For that moment, Joe felt loved and accepted the same way I felt the first time I realized Jesus loved me. Jesus found me where I was, and you too. He mastered going to the down-and-outcast.

The Lowest and the Least

The scriptures describe an awkward encounter that Jesus intentionally set in motion. On his way to Galilee, he took the disciples on a life-lesson leisure stroll to Samaria. Understand that from a geographic standpoint, it was a tad bit out of the way. Jesus was traveling from Judea to Galilee, which was miles to the north. The established route between these two cities ran to the east along the Jordan River. But Jesus did not take the established route. He needed to go to Samaria even though it was out of the way (John 4:1-4).

On a much larger scale, it would be like me trying to get from Los Angeles to Miami via Minnesota. Obviously it was not that many miles, but in those days, especially culturally speaking, it was *way* out of the way. But that is how we connect and authentically love the outcasts like Christ did—we go out of our way.

Samaria was a land of outcasts, it was the ghetto where "the Gentile dogs of people" lived. In the culture of the day, Samaritans were considered the lowest of the low. They were despised, considered dirty and unacceptable to any good Jewish person. By going through Samaria, Jesus was painting a picture of not only his willingness to go to those considered the least, but his willingness to love them regardless of what religion dictated.

Having arrived, those with Jesus grumbled and wondered why their leader was taking them to Samaria. Why would anyone go to the outcast Land of Lavender? The same reason Jesus did: to love those deemed unlovely.

Jesus sent the disciples to get some food. Unconventional in method, Jesus approached a woman at the well . . . alone. Shattering the religious rules, he spoke to her. She was alone, an outcast. Obliterating the customs and manners of the day, Jesus spoke life to her. He asked her for some water. Her response was critical and inquisitive. She wanted to know why a Jew would ask a Samarian for a drink of water—Jews shunned the outcast Samaritans. To a Jew, they were the lowest on life's ladder and the least likely to be loved.

But not to Jesus.

He invited her lover to get a drink of life too. Through the conversation, her pain and her issues with rejection, abandonment, and trust were all exposed. Jesus knew she had been divorced five times and she was with her sixth lover. Still, he offered unconditional love. She wanted a drink for her thirst and exhaustion. He offered her a drink for eternity.

He loved. When I read this story, I am astounded. I see in him everything I want to be. I see his willingness to break the mold in order to enact the miraculous.

Jesus was willing to go to the depraved of society to love. Consider her life's relational patterns:

- Samaritans were culturally and socially the lowest.
- A Samaritan woman was deemed lower.
- A divorced Samaritan woman lower still.
- A two-time divorced Samaritan woman, lower.
- A three-time divorced Samaritan woman was *still* lower.
- A *five-time* divorced Samaritan woman? She was an absolute sociological train wreck.
- Now take that same woman and shack her up with a lover? It can't get any lower than this outcast.

She wanted a drink for her thirst and exhaustion. He offered her a drink for eternity.

Jesus chose *her* to illustrate that his love has no boundaries. And he used the simplicity of a drink of water.[3]

Water for the Thirsty

Over the next year, Joe and I continued to meet. In the midst of my increased empathy, a local ministry to the gay community invited me and a few others to attend the Sacramento Gay Pride Parade. I talked to Joe about the parade, and he confirmed he would be participating. I kept my plans to myself, but I knew I would be there.

The outreach led by Char Blair of Unspoken Ministries had a simple idea that resembled the significance of what Jesus did in Samaria: show up at the parade with backpacks filled with small bottles of water labeled "Loving People for Who They Are, Not Where They Are." A small blog link pointed people to more information.

In the June heat, the parade rolled through the streets of downtown Sacramento. My friend Lance and I joined Unspoken and offered bottles of water throughout the route to anyone who was thirsty. Some women who introduced themselves to me as Butch and Bull Dyke (seriously) perched their lawn chairs next to me. For the next hour, they watched Lance and me pass out water. I can't remember anyone turning down a bottle. Some took the water, read the label, and paused. "Thank you" was all they could say. Most were stunned.

With only a few bottles left, I figured we were just about done. Little did I know a whole new world was about to open before my eyes.

Across the street from us, a red truck crept in and parked no less than fifty feet away. It was awkward to watch as the goof tried to parallel park with A-frame billboards mounted on the back of his truck.

It was what I came to call "The Hate Truck."

The truck's signs towered above the street, condemning each person. The signs were filled with judgmental statements of half truths torn from obscure, partial passages of scripture, speaking death to everyone. The driver just sat in his truck, his window cracked open. From where I was, it looked as if he was afraid to get out, so instead he slid tracts about his perspective of God through the window. They hit the ground and became soiled in the street gutter.

Butch and Bull were aggravated. They were visually upset. I was too. I never walked over to see what was on those tracts out of fear that someone would think I was with him. The tension within my soul tweaked on me—I realized that I was patient, gracious, and merciful toward those in the parade, but I felt anger toward the man who picketed the parade. Yet Jesus loves the picketer too.

With my nearly empty backpack, the two minutes that passed seemed like two decades. I finally had to break the silence with the lesbians. I cleared my throat and said, "Butch . . . Bull . . . I need to say something." They were both sipping on their nearly empty outreach bottles. I continued, cautiously choosing my words.

"I don't know where Jesus would be stationed out here in the middle of all this. But one thing I do know is that he would not be in that truck over there." I was done.

Butch took another sip. She paused and wiped the sweat from her forehead. I could see she too was thinking cautiously out of respect for our newfound friendship. She cleared her throat.

"I *can* tell you where Jesus would be," she said in a kind voice. "You are right. Jesus would not be in that Hate-mobile." She paused, as if to ensure that I was listening. "Jesus would be standing right here handing out bottles of water."

I was floored. As I turned to leave, I emotionally stumbled away as well. My mind was seared. An obvious lesbian who told me her name was Butch had just spoken direct words of encouragement to my heart. The outcast embraced me in her world. She got it. We had gone less than fifty feet when both hollered to me as Lance ran a few steps ahead. "Hey,

> **"Jesus would be standing right here handing out bottles of water."**

Preacher Boy, thank you for the water." They held their bottles up as if to say, "Cheers."

That day took me back to my coffee time with Joe. I remember he said, "Jason, do you really know what will happen when you start to reach out to this community?" I wanted to say I did, but I didn't really know. He told me. He explained that when the outcasts are loved, the religious begin to get cynical and skeptical toward the one who reached out. Essentially, he told me there would be people who would hate me for doing this. "They will begin to call you the same thing that they call us," he said. He was right.

I wish I had time to write a chapter on the hate mail we have received. I wish I had time to fully describe the social shrapnel that my senior pastor has taken for his crystal clear message of the love that Jesus has for everyone.[4]

Even though nearly two years have passed since that June parade, on any given Sunday, picketers bring their signs, posters, banners, and billboards and line the frontage road leading to our church. Sometimes there is more than one group picketing us. Ironically, it is not the folks from the Lavender District. I have joked more than once that while we passed out water, the picketers sipped on Hatorade. I know, it's totally cheesy, but after two years of this madness that has only solidified our commitment and emboldened our efforts, I can only laugh.

The picketers claim to be God-sent. They create websites and start forums that I believe are aimed to stir controversy. Again, it is laughable. On some occasions, other churches have joined them on Sunday to picket us going to church.

Newspaper articles, top stories on the evening news, blogs, podcasts—the outcasts finally are beginning to believe they have an advocate in the faith community.

The hardest thing for me is to remember that the same message that reached into a parade must reach to the side of the street where the picketers line up against us. Bless those who hate you.[5] Everyone around me is reminding me that they too are outcasts, living in the land of deception and hate. My wife said to offer grace to the religious the same way I would to the parade reveler.

Even my son offered his opinion for reaching the picketing outcast.

"Daddy, maybe you should give them a bottle of water."

Maybe he is right.

---

1. http://www.infoplease.com/us/census/data/california/sacramento/social.html.
2. http://rthoughtsrfree.org/tcnfalwell.htm#f.
3. John 4:1–26.
4. http://www.newsreview.com/sacramento/Content?oid=697201.
5. See Romans 12:14.

Jesu
Lo

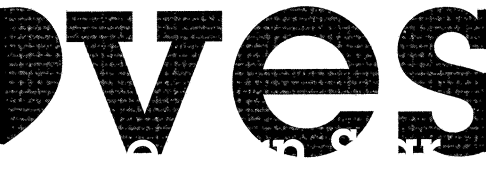

Craig

Ron Jeremy is one of today's most well-known porn stars, and I slept with him.

Let me explain.

As you hopefully have noted by now, I am not religious. In fact, I despise religion. The truth behind what drives me to despise religion while loving Jesus was Jesus' own approach. Religion produces rules and regulations to control people and bully them with the fear of hell.

Jesus was different. He outlined a set of beliefs that, if embraced, can produce a better world. Jesus made it clear that we're all sinners, and because of that equality, I can be friends with anyone. I like to surround myself with people who don't look, act, talk, or think like me.

I am on a mission. In hindsight, I never set out to connect with the porn world. But today, my mission is to help people— both the user and the producer—untangle from porn.

Seven years ago, I started a formal outreach called XXX church.com. The letters "XXX" freaked the church out, and the word "church" freaked the porn people out. The two words blended the seedy and the sacred.

Today, XXXchurch.com is the largest anti-porn website on the Internet. More than 70 million visitors have logged on since its inception. XXXchurch.com averages a half-million visitors a month—a lot for a Christian site. I think some of those hits are from people searching for naked nuns, some from a pastor or two wanting a glimpse of the former church secretary named Jessica Hahn. I have heard it all.

For the person who is addicted to viewing porn, XXX-church offers some answers. For the person who is performing, it offers some alternatives. Regardless, XXXchurch is expressing its voice of hope, connecting both with people who are *in* the industry and those messed up *by* the industry.

It's a tough road that sometimes leads me to do crazy stuff in order to build a platform to communicate that there is hope.

Porn is addictive and destructive, and prolonged exposure costs most people more than they are willing to pay. But at the same time, I am an advocate for free speech and freedom of expression, which made me a target of organized religion and at the same time embraced (with a few exceptions) by the porn industry.

Despite my willingness to speak against the effects of porn, most people in the porn industry casually embrace who I am and ignore why I do it. In the religious world, it is the opposite.

Many in the church world despise who I am and ignore what I do. It's strange, or at least ironic. Scroll through my phone and you'll find some of the top names in the adult industry. You won't find many church folks—not an indictment, just a reflection of the life I live.

Then there are the porn conventions where we pass out thousands of Bibles. During a porn trade show, people who claimed to be Christians bashed me alongside the porn stars. I explained I was there to give out Bibles that read "Jesus Loves Porn Stars" on the cover. The guy who I affectionately called "Hate Preacher" told me nobody would take the Bibles. We passed out over three thousand on the first day. Twenty-five-plus porn conventions from Australia to England to Miami to Canada to New York to Los Angeles to Las Vegas. We have handed out almost 50,000 Bibles to date, and as I write this, the team just recently returned from our first ever gay porn show. Sitting in my inbox was this email from the show promoter:

> Thank you guys for coming! Your crew was incredibly friendly and welcoming and willing to speak with anyone and everyone. We even gave them stage time in a prime slot to promote your message. Your exposure was at its peak with attendees at that time because it was our fashion show time slot. All eyes were on them and I said to your guy, (I can't remember his name sorry) that I will give them stage time as long as he doesn't get up and say "God hates gays" or anything. And he quickly assured me that you guys were not there with a message of saving our lost condemned souls, but rather to spread God's love. That stuck with me because religious organizations preach that only God is the true judge, yet have no problem protesting a funeral of a murdered hate crime victim for being gay. I'd say that is the ultimate form of judgement upon another

human being. Your message that he loves everyone and the fact that your determination to spread that word even in what I'm sure was the craziest and weirdest event and location your crew has witnessed shows me that you guys are doing a great and selfless thing. We would love to have you guys back next year! Please keep doing what you are doing. Thanks again!

Matthew

P.S. The gays thought your crew was adorable, we loved them! It was a total shock to have a bible handed to you in the midst of such debauchery.

These people have become my friends. The closest to me of all these is Ron Jeremy. I love this guy. Then there is Matthew the gay porn convention promoter, Eddie my porn producer buddy, or the countless number of porn stars we have gotten to know over the last seven years. I don't like what they do for a living. But the message of Jesus unites; it does not divide.

I can't list all the names of the people who, off the record, in a moment of authenticity, told me they wanted out. Sure, the industry would say, "Go ahead and get out," but the reality is, in many cases, the families of the performers disowned them when they started doing porn. The families say, "You have no one, and it's your fault." The porn industry says, "You have no one, and it's your fault." They have been abandoned by two groups that despise each other, yet both agree, "It is the performers' fault."

A while back, I was involved in the unthinkable. If someone had asked me in Bible college if I would ever put on

WWE wrestling tights and allow someone to body slam me, my answer would have been an emphatic NO!

Some think it is funny, some don't understand, and several have criticized me for this wrestling event. Never in a million years would I have thought to enter into a wrestling ring with the biggest man in porn, Ron Jeremy. For those of you who don't understand, WWE-style wrestling is not real. But then again, neither is porn. And to think I was wrestling Ron, how strange can it get?

King of Porn

Ron is the self-professed King of Porn.

His long scraggly hair has turned grey. It looks like it had recently been covered with a darker color, but with nearly an inch of growth, the original grey is showing. Ron Jeremy has an image to keep—he'd have to do something about that grey soon.

People may not get it, but the Porn King is friends with me, the Porn Pastor.

As a social icon birthed from a sex-crazed culture that has embraced porn, Ron Jeremy is the most popular porn star in history. His name recognition has eclipsed that of many mainstream actors.

Since the late 1970s when he broke onto the scene, his popularity has skyrocketed, and in the last few years, his career has converted to mainstream media. For Ron, the journey to the mainstream has been steady and more progressive. Planned or by accident, Ron has become—Ron is—a pop icon for the Gen-X crowd and younger. Whether he is appearing in a Kid Rock music video, making cameos in movies, or being a frequent fixture on Hollywood's red carpet, Ron is more popular now than ever.

Ron parlayed his minimal acting talent into over two thousand porno roles. Acting and directing have made him famous. As the top porn star of all time (according to *Adult Video News* magazine), Ron, a.k.a. "Hedgehog," is iconic with a cult following. When the industry realized he was willing to embrace oddity for cash, Ron was cast on VH1's *The Surreal Life*. This bizarre reality show places eight stars from various industries under one roof to live together and compete in goofy games. Former rap star Vanilla Ice and fallen televangelist Tammy Faye Baker were two of Ron's roommates. Though *The Surreal Life* was a comical reality show, viewers got to see many sides of Ron. For many people, this was their first real exposure to Ron outside of a porn plot. He's lovable, kind, courteous, and a tad whimsical.

Ron is smart, knows his industry, and will do about anything for a buck. At the same time, he is totally serious when it comes to debating porn.

What is weird is that we like each other. We are friends.

Standing on the side of the stage, dressed for a WWE match at an outreach event we created called Unscripted, I laughed as I listened to a bunch of wrestlers exiting their match. Before they were out of sight of the crowd, they high-fived and cheered compliments to the guy they had just finished throwing around the ring.

If you had been with me earlier in the Unscripted Green Room, you would have seen Ron pick me up and practice the takedown he was going to use on me. I was taken aback by his complete focus and willingness to do it over and over, making sure he did not hurt me. At the same time, he wanted to make it look real.

Showtime. As I walked toward the ring, the music blared, but I didn't hear it. The only thing going through my mind was the question of how I had gotten here. I was at an event that was entertainment, with people watching me wrestle the Porn King, Ron Jeremy. Why?

Or in reality, a better question is "Why not?" Over time, I am willing to do anything short of compromise to get the message of Jesus out! That night, people not only heard about the effects of porn, they also heard about the hope of Jesus. Ron heard it too.

As days passed after the event, I found myself looking forward to the next time I would see Ron and build on the friendship. It seemed that since we met, my progress of getting to know him better has been slowed with the stupidity of me having to answer endless emails from those thinking I should not associate with him. They would be disappointed.

> **People not only heard about the effects of porn, they also heard about the hope of Jesus.**

Days later we connected again in the D.C. area for the Great Porn Debate. Some colleges had expressed a desire to see the Porn King debate the Porn Pastor. We have only wrestled once but have debated at clubs and colleges more then thirty times over the last couple years.

Ron and celebrity agent Mike Esterman picked me up at the airport in Baltimore, and we headed to a porn debate at the University of Baltimore. Winding through the stop-

and-go travel of D.C. drive time, I pulled up my laptop and showed Ron the video clip from the wrestling match. Like a little kid seeing himself for the first time on TV, he could not get enough of it.

With Ron next to me, I realized that this was not the first time that I have been honored to impact the hurting. A few years prior, XXXchurch filmed a commercial called "Pete the Porno Puppet" with pornographer Jimmy D. The critics in Christendom wanted to lynch us. Why? I think it was because we engaged in a discussion with Jimmy D after he had written to us. Later Jimmy confessed that he had been drawn to something that intrigued him with our ministry. Our willingness to reach out caused him to also reach out. He reached out enough to volunteer his time and resources to help XXXchurch.

For me, the friendship with Jimmy was never just about the commercial. Months later and moved by the consistency of our friendship, Jimmy asked if I would officiate his daughter's wedding. Again, the critics chirped.

Jimmy D and I had become friends.

Back to the debate. The crowd was hostile, the questions were similar to debates I'd done with him in the past, and the event was sold out. Looking back, I didn't think I had made headway, but then everything changed.

Normally when he and I are on the road, it is pretty much the same routine. Ron and I each arrive, head to the debate, do the debate, go to dinner, hang out, then we fly home our separate ways. But on this night, it was different. Ron was inquisitive. Ron invited me into his world.

Scheduled to make an appearance at a new nightclub in Washington D.C., Ron invited me to join him. Hesitantly, I agreed. On the way he turned into Hooters. My heart raced and I thought to myself, *Any restaurant, but not Hooters*. So many people would use this location as a way to try finding more things wrong with what I do.

My wife and I don't frequent Hooters (although I did learn that day that kids eat free), but Mike the agent loves to eat at Hooters. *Great*, I thought. *He invited me to go deeper and I am going to have to say, "No thank you, their T-shirts are too tight."* Or do I choose to take a step deeper into a place that is 90 percent legendary in its level of madness. Remember: kids eat free.

I had a decision to make. Do I sit in the car on a pile of pity? Do I ask them to drop me off at the restaurant across the street while they eat? Do I alienate myself from this guy who has become a friend by saying, "I'd love to eat with you; I just can't do it here."

What do I do?

What would you do?

What would Jesus do?

I don't know what you would do, but I went inside. We sat down and shared a meal. The crowds followed just like they do at any restaurant with Ron. All the waitresses, the manager, the supervisor, everyone in a Hooters uniform, at some point, interrupted our dinner and wanted a photo with their camera phone. I ended up taking the pictures.

In between crowds, a lady approached the table. She was a waitress who was not working but had dropped in to pick up her paycheck, a little boy in tow. He looked to be nine or ten. She asked Ron for a photo, and I ended up taking the photo of the three of them. Then she said, "Can you take one of just Ron and my son?" Why would a mom want a picture of her little boy and the King of Porn? I can't answer that. All I know is, it hurt.

I slipped away to the bathroom. As I stood over the sink, my stomach sank. I looked into the mirror stained by water spots and I just began to pray.

"God . . . this man . . . this woman and her son, God . . ."

When I don't know what to say, I pray. I wonder what it would have been like to hang out with Jesus. What would it have been like to join him for dinner and watch the circus around him? It had to have been chaos. His choice of company created critics all around him. I think of Zacchaeus, who had Jesus over for dinner. Jesus ignored his critics and joined him, inviting himself into Zacchaeus's world.

> **I wonder what it would have been like to hang out with Jesus.**

Porn King vs. Porn Pastor

In the midst of prepping for the wrestling match, the D.C. trip, and a massively promoted Porn Debate Tour, a pastor friend of mine, Don Golden, told me, "All you can do with Ron is keep inviting him into your world." He was talking about the biblical mandate where Jesus instructed his followers to go into the entire world and communicate hope.[1] The Bible calls this mandate the Great Commission.

I call it my only job on this planet.

Don explained that the whole purpose of my connection to Ron was just that: an opportunity to connect. It was less about preaching to people and calling them to a confession and more about inviting hurting and unknowing people into our world. It is about sharing with them your friends, family, and beliefs, over time.

That gave me a new outlook. That excited me. Ron is open to experiencing my world. He has met my family, my friends, and pastor friends of mine. He has accepted me because I accepted him. He invited me into his world.

Beyond Hooters, what will be my ongoing response?

How far do you go?

Is it a give-and-take relationship with him?

Is it is a trade-for-trade arrangement?

Ron didn't invite me to dinner to try to drag me down or trip up my life's story. He invited me to dinner at a restaurant, just like I have done with him.

Is there a line? Sure. But dinner at Hooters didn't cross it for me.

When I returned from my impromptu prayer vigil in the bathroom, Ron was being bombarded with more fans. The question we kept answering at Hooters was, "What are you doing tonight in Maryland?" Our answer: "We are doing a debate tonight on the issue of pornography." Sometimes he spoke. Other times I spoke. The strange part was that everyone wanted to know who the opponent was. They were repeatedly surprised when Ron pointed across the table at me.

In our world of belief, most opponents don't gather for dinner together before a match. I guess that is the first lesson I learned that night. I discovered I would rather be his friend than his opponent. Christians have way too many opponents. I am a Christian. Yet I think for comfort's sake, Christians become too safe and choose to gather together in small groups, or holy huddles, hoping "the world" doesn't get in.

I've seen how many have turned exclusive in Bible circles, ironically, ignoring the Bible's message of an all-inclusive love. These groups devise game plans and strategies for reaching the opponent; they have come up with emergent lingo, which many on the same team do not even understand. If those within the church exclude each other, whether knowingly or accidentally, imagine how those outside the church must feel.

Closer Than They Appear

Jesus said, "Love your neighbor . . . love your enemy . . . just love, because I love." Jesus loved and spent time with people who appeared to be far from belief. In reality, many in the adult industry are hurting and ready to make a change. Some just don't how to make a connection to Jesus. We can only tell them how if we are close to them. It is in this proximity that we realize many are closer to walking with Jesus than they appear.

Consider Jesus' words to Zacchaeus: "Hey, Zacchaeus, tonight I am coming to your house for dinner."[2]

Jesus stunned the disciples by his willingness to dine with the dirty. Jesus did not have an argument to win. He just loved. Those disagreements, the points we think we need to prove, those sins we think we need to call out—Jesus said, "I didn't come to judge." He came to love. That condemning style has created deaf ears.

After the dinner, my friend Jonathan joined up with me, and we headed back to the D.C. club. We were taken to the back of the club. We were given special "ALL ACCESS, VIP, Ron Jeremy" lanyards and ushered into a crowded scene. It was approaching midnight.

I have two kids and a wife. Jonathan has three kids and a wife. The lanyard made people assume I was part of the team. Looking down at my frail size, they knew I was not security.

Photos, autographs, you name it, Ron posed. I stood off to the side but was part of his world. I watched the crowd slowly fade. Eventually, Ron sat at an empty couch, exhausted, and the party was over. I knew the craziness would only last a few hours. It would eventually come to an end. It is all temporary—the fame, the sex, the girls, the life—and eventually it all will go away. Not just for Ron; for everyone. And then what?

First John 2:15–17 says, "Stop loving the evil world and all it has to offer, for the world offers the craze for sex, ambition to buy everything you see, and pride that comes from being wealthy or important. The world is fading away quickly along with everything it craves, but if you do the will of God you will live forever" (TLB).

By 2:30 a.m. the club was empty. When all the glitz and glamour were gone, a friend with faith was what was left. As Ron's weary eyes fought to stay open, the picture of us there together spoke of faith, hope, and love.

After we were done hanging out, I gave back my all-access pass and headed back to the hotel. I realized we were on the same team. I did not need the lanyard anymore to see that.

We leave our differences regarding porn, though apparent, at the debate podium. In life, Ron Jeremy cannot be my opponent. He must be a friend. Friends share friends and invite each other into their world. We're more alike than we are different. We both have struggles, we both have challenges. We both are in need of a Savior who loves.

How are you and I different? If you are a person who has yet to understand that Jesus loves you, I would call you a pre-Christian. How do you perceive Christians?

As the years have passed, I realize I love to be around pre-Christians. On the other hand, some Christians make me feel awkward. They offer their opinions when no one asked for them. They set in motion a swirling debate of how I should live my life. Most of the standards that are slung at me are darts. The darts are man-made and in many cases try to corral me into a box of beliefs that dictate the depth of how or where I can express my story.

I'll just be honest. Sometimes it feels like, because of their own spiritual insecurity, they demand that *my* faith look like *their* faith. They demand that I go and love only where they approve.

After completing the debate in D.C. with Ron, we realized that we could do this in a bunch of cities. So recently, a group of friends and I gathered at my old home in Grand Rapids, Michigan. We sat like schoolchildren on the floor with our legs crossed. For the ten of us, we were on the doorstep of what was a scientific laboratory of love. Though I knew everyone in the room, the diverse group needed to introduce themselves.

> **We're more alike than we are different. . . . We both are in need of a Savior who loves.**

Each person was unique. Some of XXXchurch's interns were there. My wife was there, more or less to keep my kids from taking over the meeting. Jason had just landed from Sacramento. Each of us came from a different background; all of us represented the same motive: to love. For me, I wanted to love Ron and communicate hope to him.

We planned The Porn Debate Tour. For seven consecutive nights, we would travel to cities and host an event where Ron and I would debate. What was interesting was the response of each guest. I saw apprehension. I saw excitement. They were about to have their Hooter-type moment. Not at my house, but on the road. Let me explain.

The debate would work. I had seen Ron in action and knew that we had chemistry. But I needed these friends on the bus to pull this off, and I didn't know how they would act around, respond to, or treat Ron. My heart knew that they would be loving and accepting, but my conscience would not allow me to load this bus without first prepping them with a pep talk on inclusion.

I remember my words vividly: "Ron may do some things, say some things, or even show some things that you are not going to agree with. Ron may ignore you. He may challenge you. His vocabulary could offend you. But we all must remember the purpose of having one bus rather than two. We are going to look at Ron the way Jesus sees him. The pastor and porn star can coexist with purpose."

Everyone listened carefully. Emotions were raw. Each person had given up their own time, taken vacation, left his or her families, in order to love.

Slowly, I did my best to motivate.

"Regardless of what you see, love him. Regardless of what you expect, love. Regardless of what you will tolerate, remember, tolerance is not compromise. Tolerance gives us the platform and relational equity to be there."

I saw in their eyes that each was getting it. We stopped only ten minutes in and—like I had prayed in the Hooter's bathroom for the mom, her son, and Ron—I asked that we take a moment to pray together. The prayers were simple and yet profound. There was no one to impress. There was no one in the grandstands, just a roomful of people who knew love could make a difference.

Ripped for Reaching Ron

Loaded and barreling down the road, we were about to have Ron join us. In addition to those who gathered in my home, joining me on the trip was my family. My wife, Jeanette, and my two kids, Nolan and Elise, ages four and two at the time, took the bunks closest to the front of the bus. Jeanette seemed to think this was the farthest from the back of the bus, and if anything were going to go down, it would probably be in the back.

As I watched her tuck my kids into their beds, so many thoughts clogged my mind. For weeks leading up to this event, I was bombarded with questions I expected to hear. Questions like, Are you scared for your kids? What about your wife? Is Ron Jeremy going to make any money off ticket sales? Why should I come to the debate to hear Ron's side of the story? Do you guys only have one bus? Are you okay promoting a porn star?

Among those who heard what we were doing and decided to voice their concern was a guy we'll call Tim, who emailed to give his two cents on how I should proceed. This is what his email said:

Jesus said that the person who promotes sin, if I understand the verse right, a guy like Ron, would be better off if he tied a millstone around his neck and flung himself into a lake. Jesus was very stern with the person that stumbles a child of God into sin—like the pornography promoter. Although Ron's conversion would be a really great miracle of God, I think you might be wasting the small amount of time you have available on him. He's promoting porn. He's made his decision and he's proselytizing others to join him in his beliefs.

Sadly, Tim represents so many people. They believe Ron is a waste of time. They believe that others who don't look like or believe like them are not worth the time. Tim stated that Jesus was very stern. I agree. But I disagree as to where the stern Savior was directing his emotion. I see Jesus growing weary of sentiments like those expressed by Tim.

In the earlier chapters of his life, Jesus was surrounded by those who were in the process of discovery. His life painted a clear picture of how to deal with the embezzling crook named Zack, a blind man, a lowly adulteress, a prostitute, and so many others. He loved those who didn't look, act, think, talk, or even believe like him or *in* him.

With deceived religionists like Tim, I don't even know what to say. His lack of inclusion is the very thing that has prevented people like Ron from considering faith. Ron was quick to point this out. In one of the debates, he was asked about faith. After a long rabbit trail that Ron raced down, he finally nailed it. He said that I, as a pastor, would be more embraced by the porn industry than he would be at a church.

I am not one to doubt many things. I have what some would call a blind faith. When presented with a mountain-sized challenge or project, I am the first person in my crowd to say, "Yes, let's do it." I tend to only ask questions later on, and only if things are not working.

I continue to be amazed by God. Every day I am blown away that I get to be a part of something that is significant. I get to show Ron that Jesus loves him.

I am not the best guy for the job, especially this one. I feel inadequate; yet, I am realizing that this is a subtle job with no outline. During the porn debate tour as I loaded the bus one day, a former employee looked square in my eyes and said the oddest thing to me: "Make sure to get it done."

It sounded to me like a coach was talking to his quarterback prior to having to throw a long pass to win the game. I know he meant well. But the words sounded strange to me, as if something I could say would change the results of the eternity already on hold for Ron. Yes, I could speak love to Ron, but Jesus is the only one who would, could, did, or will change his heart.

When this guy finished his pep talk, I smiled. In the back of my mind, I thought for a moment. I realized what it was all about. Or better, what it was not about. It was not about cornering Ron on the debate stage. It was not to get Ron to leave porn. It was about love.

The tour wasn't about *what I say* to Ron, it's more about *what I don't say*.

Ron brought the swingers on the bus while my children were sleeping . . . I said nothing. When Ron moved into the green room backstage with girls surrounding him . . . I said nothing.

When Ron was nowhere to be found five minutes before the debate started . . . I said nothing.

Others questioned us. Our families, our friends, they asked, "What did you sign up for?" What would happen when a pastor and his family stepped on a tour bus with the biggest porn star in the country?

I know what I signed up for. It was not a debate. It was not a tour. It was a chance to exhibit the love of Jesus to Ron. My friend Paul sent me an email during the trip to remind me of that.

He said, "Dude, be Jesus to Ron. You may be the closest thing to Jesus he's ever seen. Just be Jesus to him, no matter how hard it might sometimes be."

Paul's challenge was a big one. Faith-filled, at that. Craig Gross like Jesus . . . not a chance!

Would Jesus laugh at Ron's jokes? Probably not. Would Jesus swear when he got upset? No. Would Jesus even take part in a porn debate? I don't know. But what I do know is that Jesus would be on that bus.

Jesus would have served Ron on the tour. Jesus would have shuttled him around to the interviews, dinner, and back again. My wife's "Soccer Mom" minivan was converted into the "Porn King Tour Taxi." Jesus would have driven!

Jesus showed up as consistent love to Ron. He was braided into our conversations. He was woven through our discussions. He was evident as determination and patience in our exhaustion. He was the fabric and purpose of the Porn Debate Tour, not just in conversation, but also in a consistent illustration. He was there.

So many conversations opened my mind to Ron's vantage point and view of the world. Rolling down the highway toward Chicago, Ron told me that he believed the truest form of love is when a couple grows old together. He said love is at its strongest when one person can't live without the other person. He described the evident picture of love in the story of Johnny Cash and June Carter. Ron was moved by the love they had for each other. When June died, though Johnny was in reasonably good health, he died shortly after.

Ron Jeremy was telling us that this is the truest form of love. Why? It's what he wants so badly, yet it's what he is most afraid of. Ron's picture of love is very similar to the one Jesus offers: "I love so others can live."

Will Ron ever experience and completely understand that love?

A few nights later on our drive to Pittsburgh, *CNN Headline News* called. They wanted Ron and me for a live segment. They booked us in two separate studios to do the live feed. Walking through the local affiliate, Ron and I thought this was strange. Why would they put us in separate rooms for the recording? Why? Because we were debating porn and we have different opinions. They did not think we could be in the same studio together. Little did CNN know that each night Ron bunked near my family and me, just steps away on the same bus.

The world divides.

Jesus unites.

The world expects differences to get in the way of friend-ships. Religion, and even more specifically the Christian in-stitution called "church," is known for thinking they are right and everyone else is wrong. The church expects people who do not subscribe to their tenets to somehow find their way into the sanctuary. They expect the Rons of this world to come inside, but only once they figure out they're "lost."

The world divides.

Jesus unites.

Not the case with Jesus. He said, "I have come for the sick. The healthy do not need a doctor."[3]

Back on the tour bus, Ron and I laughed. We watched the replay of the CNN interview. He told me I did well.

Now that the tour is over, I realize the real story was not about porn. That is not why I boarded that bus. CNN missed it, but I know the hundreds of people who saw us each night did not miss it. They could not miss the camaraderie we shared.

We are friends.

Ron Jeremy is my friend.

Will he leave porn?

Will he come to know the Lord?

What if he already has?

I don't know. What really matters are neither the ques-tions nor the answers. What really matters is this: Ron, Jesus loves you.

♥

A team of three independent filmmakers traveled on the bus with us over the seven-day trip. Their documentary on the Porn Debate Tour is called Master Debaters *and can be found online at www.masterdebaters.tv.*

---

1. Matthew 28:18–20.
2. See Luke 19:1–9.
3. See Mark 2:17.

Jesu
Lo

Craig

The darker the place, the more Jesus' truth shines, and in Vegas, where I live, his truth shines even brighter than the lights of the strip. Jesus transcends differences and connects with compassion. When Jason and I started this journey, we ventured into some of these dark corners. Both of us were committed to model, or at least *try* to model, the love Christ had for people.

But when we really looked, we found an additional subculture that needed to be loved. We had overlooked the obvious: Jesus loves the religious.

Most people would define *religion* as the institution that teaches others the pursuit of a higher deity, but I would call that a *faith community*. I prefer to define religion as a stale presentation of tradition that has drifted from truth, as man's naturalizing of the supernatural. It is trying to make predictable the spontaneous. It is the strangulation of the spiritual. It is the act of crucifying Jesus again because he stepped beyond rules and regulations and focused on relationships with people.

Jesus metaphorically took the laws of man and nailed them to the cross he died on. He said love is now the law, and the one who does not love has transgressed the greatest law of them all.

Religion kills; relationship gives life. Religion sets up regulations and makes them into habitual, boring routines that look to the external and ignore the heart. For the religious, it can become an outward persona that fuels fraud.

Religion's purest definition comes down to finger pointing. Essentially, if I can tend to other people's business, if I can find and point out the dirt on *others*, then *my* dirt will be overlooked. If I can judge others, then *I* must be spiritual.

Jesus said that only God judges. So how can we judge? And yet, judgment is abundant.

We saw it in so many places while traveling and writing. For example, during our bus tour with Ron Jeremy and my family, along with a few other friends, we were blasted by the religious for being near Ron. Ron saw it and often said, "My world loves you more than your world loves me." Sad, but true.

On many nights after the debate, we were greeted by people who had just heard me make a crystal clear presentation of redemption through Christ, and I can't remember a single time when a secularist verbally accosted me. Oh, they disagreed, and though some of them did not accept my belief, they at least affirmed it. Hostility was absent. Hatred was abandoned. We had expected heated confrontations with the unchurched and the secularists we were going to encounter, but they never materialized.

But there were heated confrontations on other fronts . . .

Skateboard Cross

As the tour bus rolled into Indianapolis, the blistering 100-plus temperature, complete with energy-sucking humidity, foreshadowed the events of the evening. We had booked the venue without looking at it first, and we found it to be drab and dilapidated. It was embarrassing to think people had bought tickets to sit in a broken-down brick building without a cooling system. We packed hundreds of people in and tried desperately to cool the hot air by moving it with fans we'd bought from Home Depot. It wasn't the best beginning.

Ron and I had been verbally jousting in the tour bus over his continual habit of casually strolling in thirty minutes late to meetings, as if on this day he did not care about the fact that hundreds had paid to hear him argue. His industry friends had shown up night after night. I would not be surprised if they had hammered him for being on a bus with a bunch of Christians.

I stepped off the bus sixty minutes before showtime and caught a glimpse of the line of people snaking around the building and down the block. I also saw a different group of people patrolling up and down the street in clear view. They had come with their own agenda: to disrupt, confront, and divide.

A couple of guys had built a wooden cross and attached a single skateboard wheel to the bottom of it for ease of transport. Draped over one of their shoulders, the wooden cross—a timeless image of freedom and hope—was being used to imprison our efforts and derail our discussion. I wanted to count their progress as they made laps around the building, but instead I had to get away from them. Though they blasted our tour bus as a den of debauchery, I doubt they knew that, besides Ron, it was filled with pastors and other ministers of the gospel.

Throughout the trip, Ron and Jason had engaged in many good conversations about Christianity. I debated Ron, kept the tour pressing forward, did the press interviews, and offered him statements of encouragement. Jason was on the tour working the crowd each night as the debate moderator. Onstage he played no favorites. But on the bus when there was downtime, Jason talked to Ron at length about the scriptures. Halfway through the trip, Ron figured out Jason was a pastor.

> **Though they blasted our tour bus as a den of debauchery, I doubt they knew that, besides Ron, it was filled with pastors and other ministers of the gospel.**

Before I had stepped off the bus to the cross guys, I had tossed Ron a copy of our "Jesus Loves Porn Stars" New Testament.

Look at the picture that was snapped in this moment. There are three vantage points to consider:

1. **The unchurched gathered:** A crowd lined the streets; they'd purchased tickets to hear a debate about adult content but would discover absolutes about Christ.
2. **The porn star and pastor discussed scripture:** Inside the bus, I had tossed Ron the scriptures, and he picked them up and started to read them.

3. **The religious judged the intent and efforts of our outreach:** The cross-rolling religionists told us why we were no better than the "perverts of the industry we debated."

Ron read. The religious judged. I fumed.

And Jesus loved. He loved both sides.

If I'm being totally honest, I was angry. I wanted to try to talk logically, but I had lost all patience. I really felt like this could be the straw of insignificant weight that could potentially collapse my resilience and tenacity.

In the midst of all this, Jason had placed a call to his senior pastor, Rick Cole. By sheer coincidence, Jason remembered Rick was visiting Indianapolis for their denomination's National Council Meeting.[1] Half joking, Jason asked Rick if he wanted to attend the porn debate instead of the council meeting and see firsthand the outreach that was occurring. Rick was in.

Rick showed up and sat in the second row, and it was the shot in the arm, the snapshot for my soul, that I needed to get beyond the acidic taste that had formed in my mouth regarding so many in the church—not the entire church world, just the parts that are ingrown.

Rick represented what I am drawn to in Christian leadership. He was willing to forego a gathering of thousands of denominational leaders discussing business-as-usual to venture into the heat-afflicted air of the gutter where hurting and broken humanity waited.

After the debate, Jason and Rick slipped into PF Chang's in downtown Indianapolis. Swirling around them was a slice of the ordained clergy that were in town for the conference. Rick and Jason sat discussing the debate, and Jason explained it had been a great week of dialogue, but he was feeling the effects of being on the bus. But after nearly an hour of observing and overhearing the conversations of the convention that bled over to their table, Jason wanted to go back to the bus.

Rick was willing to forego a gathering of thousands of denominational leaders discussing business-as-usual to venture into the heat-afflicted air of the gutter where hurting and broken humanity waited.

Rick had breathed the pastoral life into Jason that he needed to be refueled. But between the porn-debate bus and the pastor's denominational convention, Jason chose the bus. Had the option been given to him, Rick probably would have too.

Love Reaches ALL

Whether it was with the Samaritan woman, the adulterous woman, the wedding at Cana, or a host of other occurrences, Jesus invested time and truth in environments that made the religious cringe. When Jesus headed to the house of Zacchaeus, the religious said, "What business does he have getting cozy with this crook?"[2]

As I write this, over a year has passed since that night in Indianapolis. But it wasn't until Jason and I inked this manuscript that we realized something dangerous had occurred inside us. In many ways we had become a slice of the very thing we despised. We had been judgmental toward judgmental people.

We are skeptics of smooth-talking TV preachers. We are jaded against the portrayal of some television presentations of Christianity. Yet Jesus loves those people, too, and the people who watch them. Love reaches ALL people.

When we reflected on the tone of the previous chapters, we noticed two prevailing threads we'd woven to hold this book together. At times those threads were twisted so tightly, braided and blended so concisely, it was hard to decipher where one started and where the other ended.

The main thread of truth was stitched in a patch called "Savior" that covers the blotched mistakes of humanity. Essentially, this whole book was created to speak life and hope, encouragement and redemption.

But after reading and rereading it, we discovered a second thread: the thread of tainted love. Jason and I both love the church. Yet we realize that our love is tainted by our response to the actions of those who have placed tradition above truth. In a sense, we failed to realize that these are still people whom God loves. These are people who, because of their insecurities, uncertainties, and ignorance, have missed the mark by a universe. The same way I miss it. The same way Jason, Ron, Rick, or any other person misses it.

Not one of us is perfect.[3] Only Jesus was perfect, and that is what makes the statement "Jesus loves you" so profound.[4] It is eternal and all-encompassing.

When I flip through television stations with religious content, my head swirls with its two pervasive messages. On one side, we have constant communication about cash and prosperity; on the other side, we see a theme of judgment that ostracizes people who may be on a search for God. And it seems like the more preachers yell, the more the crowd says, "Amen!"

Pompous preachers parade with ringmaster tactics mesmerizing[5] the crowd into a trancelike state. Hours are spent "breathing in" God, often without ever breathing him out to humanity. Many good people spend hours tuned into TV preachers who call themselves evangelists, but I often wonder if those preachers ever reach beyond the coffers and into the community of hurting humanity.

An evangelist is not someone who runs through a crowded airport of thousands of unchurched, pre-Christian people to fly to a Christian television station to preach to a studio audience of Christian people. An evangelist meets the hurting where they are; whether they encounter wayward, rebellious, or even hedonistic people, evangelists connect and communicate Christ's unfailing love.

When the religious gather and form ingrown circles, they are not fulfilling the Great Commission. They simply are not. The members of the holy huddle must disperse and dedicate themselves to the single most important message of the Bible: Jesus loves and saves.

At times my disgust is rooted in thinking, *But people watching this stuff should know better*.

A clear picture of Christ is not always clear when people unfamiliar with church culture see snapshots of televised sermons. To those who are unknowledge-

> **The members of the holy huddle must disperse and dedicate themselves to the single most important message of the Bible: Jesus loves and saves.**

able, the content and how it is presented is totally foreign. For Jesus, it was not about more offerings, private jets, or lavish lifestyles. Jesus made it clear. It is about love.

When our heads are shaking in disgust, we realize that it is a few examples that can spoil the great intentions of many. This is not a broad-stroke generalization, it is the perception that many unchurched have of organized religion that has been defined by what they see on television. If the goal is to "reach the world," the world should not be repelled by what they see spoken about Jesus. But many are.

But even Jesus said, "Father, forgive them, for they don't know what they are doing."[6] He modeled what I should do. Those raised around the church *should* know better. They should realize that the message of Christ is what we are called to emulate, but I also have to reframe my perspective. I need to understand that they too are on a journey.

Think about the many pervasive messages of the pulpit in the eighties. As a kid growing up during those years, I heard voices like Jimmy Swaggart and Jerry Falwell, the birth of the Moral Majority—it seemed to me that these entities decided which group to bash. So, casual followers in the church did what they saw modeled. They judged. They picked and chose which sins to make the focus: abortion, homosexuality, etc. They made those issues their banner cry, all the while forgetting that *their* mission was supposed to be *Jesus'* mission.

The rules of the game changed, and many Christians did what they felt was the right thing to do, what they saw coming out of the pulpits. In reality, it looked nothing like the Jesus in the synagogue found in scripture.

Jesus returned to Galilee in the power of the Spirit, and news about him spread through the whole countryside. He taught in their synagogues, and everyone praised him.

He went to Nazareth, where he had been brought up, and on the Sabbath day he went into the synagogue, as was his custom. And he stood up to read. The scroll of the prophet Isaiah was handed to him. Unrolling it, he found the place where it is written:

"The Spirit of the Lord is on me, because he has anointed me to preach good news to the poor. He has sent me to proclaim freedom for the prisoners and recovery of sight for the blind, to release the oppressed, to proclaim the year of the Lord's favor."

Then he rolled up the scroll, gave it back to the attendant and sat down. The eyes of everyone in the synagogue were fastened on him, and he began by saying to them, "Today this scripture is fulfilled in your hearing."

All spoke well of him and were amazed at the gracious words that came from his lips.

Luke 4:14–22

Only moments later, they turned on him as he continued to explain his mission.

All the people in the synagogue were furious when they heard this. They got up, drove him out of the town, and took him to the brow of the hill on which the town was built, in order to throw him down the cliff. But he walked right through the crowd and went on his way.

Luke 4:28–30

Jesus was trying to dissect a clear picture of love and who was included in it. To add punch to his purpose, he quoted from the Old Testament prophet, a person the religious should have respected. But it only inflamed them.

They didn't get the message. Jesus' love was to deliver life.

What would it look like if every Christian and church were to communicate good news to the poor?

What would happen if we constantly proclaimed freedom for the prisoners, both physically and spiritually?

What if we were more concerned about the physically afflicted? In this case, it was the recovery of sight for the blind, but what if it was cancer, leukemia, AIDS, or any other ailment?

What if we worked to better others? Looking for ways to release the oppressed, we would make a great difference!

What if all of these things were delivered as hope? We would be proclaiming not judgment but the favor of the Lord.

I find myself wanting to advocate justice for the hurting and pronouncing judgment on the religious. In this, I have become the very thing I despise. My cynical approach toward "Churchianity" only bolsters their claims against us.

I am quick to offer grace to the rebellious and wayward. But I am slow in offering it to the religious, if I offer it at all. Yet I must.

1. The church's pastoral leadership of their denomination meets every other year in different cities to discuss business items, vision, and connect with other pastors. Rick Cole had flown in for this gathering the day before the debate and stayed two additional days after we had moved to the next city.

2. Luke 19:7 Message: "Everyone who saw the incident was indignant and grumped, 'What business does he have getting cozy with this crook?'"

3. Romans 3:23–24: "For all have sinned and fall short of the glory of God, and are justified freely by his grace through the redemption that came by Christ Jesus."

4. Romans 5:8: "But God demonstrates his own love for us in this: While we were still sinners, Christ died for us."

5. "Mesmerizing" (adj.), attracting and holding interest as if by a spell; (verb) to spellbind, enthrall (Dictionary.com). In short, the word is taken from the name Franz Mesmer who was thought to be able to hypnotize and then magnetically draw people in.

6. Luke 23:34 NLT.

Jesu
Lo

ls

oves

The   Kn w

Craig

Jason and I both wrestle with the complexities of a life dedicated to vocational ministry. Many times, the people and situations that we engage in are complex. Our ultimate goal is to tell as many people as possible that Jesus is who he said he is and he loves unconditionally. When we are invited into the world of those who have yet to believe, many within faith communities question our motives, sanity, and commitment. The further we venture into the secular world with a message of hope, the more skeptical some within the church become.

There are times we have been so angry at injustice and so frustrated at tradition that we have walked away, at least mentally, from organized church. But in our hearts and in our minds, we always know we will come back.

There are things that happen within organized religion and denominationalism that make everything seem worthless. There are times when our actions have been filled with such hypocrisy that we wondered if anyone would or should even listen. We have hit the wall in our ministries where we have reconsidered if we should keep doing what we do.

Jason has thought about it a lot. There are times when he has wanted to escape the pressures that come along with working fifteen years at a megachurch. Random thoughts have occasionally flown through his mind. There are thoughts that nearly convinced him to go out and be The Cable Guy full time. Other times, he has been offered big money and even bigger platforms, but it would be in Corporate America, and that's not where he feels called. His mind and heart argue, without a clear answer sometimes; he is left feeling like he just doesn't know.

I am faced with it daily. I wonder about whether or not we are doing everything we can at XXXchurch to reach the corrupted conscience, both in the church and in the adult industry. I face the uncertainty of funding to keep our message viable in the billion-dollar porn industry. We don't try to compete, but we have seen in years past that when we market well, we reach an unreached group with greater impact and efficiency. There are constant battles with media, haters, religionists—sometimes a combination of all three. Like Jason, sometimes I just don't know. We often recalibrate and try to format a plan to navigate through the traditions of man and the truths of God. It gets sticky sometimes.

Both of us are committed to reaching people with the hope of Jesus. We want people to find wholeness and purpose. We want to live our lives to the fullest. We both want to go full speed ahead. Only a few things really mess up our forward traction.

When we see people acting contrary to Jesus' mission, it messes us up, because we do it too. When we face resistance, it also motivates us. But in reality, it messes up everyone who has a genuine concern for humanity. When Christians do stupid things, it affects us too; the unchurched world takes a step back and reconsiders. They look at our lives, our values, our ethics, and our motives, and decide if faith is of value. When there is an inconsistency between our behavior and our beliefs, confusion prevails.

They like Jesus, they just don't like the church.

We have talked to thousands of unchurched/pre-Christian people, and a high percentage of them say they aren't interested in Christianity because of Christian behavior. As writer Dan Kimball explains, they like Jesus, they just don't like the church.[1]

Haven for Hypocrisy?

In frustration I have heard many say, "I don't go to church because it is filled with a bunch of hypocrites." The inconsistent behavior makes them unsure of their beliefs.

What can we be sure of? What has been pedaled down through the centuries as tradition? What truth is being overlooked? Can I trust that what I believe can stand up against scrutiny?

Jesus Loves You, THIS I KNOW!

Can my faith land on some solid fact? Can I trust there is more to this faith than subjective anecdotes? Can I look at history, science, and mathematics, and courageously proclaim, "This I know"?

The answer? An emphatic yes!

Yet at the same time, no one will ever be able to prove God. Although his works are seen in our everyday existence, his hand is evident in infinite probabilities, and the scriptures provide evidence, these are still not absolute proof.

But that is why it is called faith. It is the ability to embrace the things hoped for but not yet seen.[2]

Jason and I have tried to lay aside all the cumbersome things that really don't matter in the long run. Essentially, we have both committed to majoring on the majors and letting the minor things slip away. We refuse to be crippled by a set of rules and regulations. Instead we've landed on loving God with all of our heart, mind, soul, and strength. We have landed on loving our neighbors even as our own family.

As you have read, we have staked a lot on a deep-rooted belief that Jesus is who he said he is and he will do all he promised to do. We believe that Jesus claimed to be God, setting him apart from every other world religious leader. Never has a leader claimed to be God and have the ability in his own power to forgive sins. Jesus did.

We are fully committed to the truth found in the cross. It is essential. There are many other opinions on how one may be atoned. But this I know: redemption is guaranteed through a relationship with Jesus. Jesus made it very clear with an audacious claim: No person can get to God except through him.[3] When I'm asked how he could make such a claim, my response is, "An audacious claim is the result of an audacious Christ who climbed up on a cross and brought God and man together, joining their

Never has a leader claimed to be God and have the ability in his own power to forgive sins. Jesus did.

hands and then declaring the separation was over. He said it this way: 'It is finished.' "

Scripture Speaks

Jason and I find great comfort and truth in the fact that after Jesus died on the cross, he was placed in a tomb. Just as was predicted, on day three, Jesus rose to life. In doing so, he secured life for you and me. All of Christianity hinges on this singular historical event: this I know. All of my eggs are in this basket. If the resurrection of Christ were disproved, it would put me out of business. This I know! My whole ministry is built on that singular historical fact.

We both are committed to the imminent return of Jesus. We do not believe that it is a "pie in the sky," weak excuse for belief. We do not spend hours debating fellow believers on whether that return will occur pre-tribulation, mid-tribulation, or post-tribulation. While fellow believers argue that to no avail, we want to reach out and love the unlovely. This I know.

When we discuss faith with those who seek to be antagonistic, we refuse to be trapped in an unwinnable situation. Instead, we seek common ground, try to remain civil, and yet continue to live life in a passionate pursuit of God. This assures that we are seeking to become the best version of ourselves, the version that God created in his image.

When things get bad, we can stake a claim and declare, "This I know!"

I KNOW

... he sticks closer than a brother.

A man of many companions may come to ruin, but there is a friend who sticks closer than a brother. *Proverbs 18:24*

... he will never leave or forsake you.

Be strong and courageous. Do not be afraid or terrified because of them, for the LORD your God goes with you; he will never leave you nor forsake you. *Deuteronomy 31:6*

Those who know your name will trust in you, for you, LORD, have never forsaken those who seek you. *Psalm 9:10*

... he chose you.

You did not choose Me, but I chose you, and appointed you that you would go and bear fruit, and that your fruit would remain, so that whatever you ask of the Father in My name He may give to you. *John 15:16 NASB*

Just as He chose us in Him before the foundation of the world, that we would be holy and blameless before Him. In love He predestined us to adoption as sons through Jesus Christ to Himself, according to the kind intention of His will. *Ephesians 1:4–5 NASB*

I KNOW

... you have a safe place.

As for God, His way is blameless; the word of the LORD is tried; He is a shield to all who take refuge in Him. *Psalm 18:30 NASB*

The LORD helps them and delivers them; He delivers them from the wicked and saves them, because they take refuge in Him. *Psalm 37:40 NASB*

... I am not condemned but loved.

Therefore, there is now no condemnation for those who are in Christ Jesus. *Romans 8:1*

God did not send the Son into the world to judge the world, but that the world might be saved through Him. He who believes in Him is not judged; he who does not believe has been judged already, because he has not believed in the name of the only begotten Son of God. *John 3:17 NASB*

... he is with you in the midst of hardship.

Even though I walk through the valley of the shadow of death, I fear no evil, for You are with me; Your rod and Your staff, they comfort me. *Psalm 23:4 NASB*

Blessed are those who mourn, for they shall be comforted. *Matthew 5:4 NASB*

... he will provide for you.

God is able to make all grace abound to you, so that always having all sufficiency in everything, you may have abundance for every good deed. *2 Corinthians 9:8 NASB*

The young lions do lack and suffer hunger; but they who seek the LORD shall not be in want of any good thing. *Psalm 34:10 NASB*

... he is watching over you.

He will not allow your foot to slip; He who keeps you will not slumber. Behold, He who keeps Israel will neither slumber nor sleep. *Psalm 121:3–4 NASB*

... nothing can separate you from his love.

For I am convinced that neither death, nor life, nor angels, nor principalities, nor things present, nor things to come, nor powers, nor height, nor depth, nor any other created thing, will be able to separate us from the love of God, which is in Christ Jesus our Lord. *Romans 8:38–39 NASB*

... even when I can't forgive myself, he has forgiven me.

That through His name everyone who believes in Him receives forgiveness of mistakes. *Acts 10:43 NASB*

He has not dealt with us according to our sins, nor rewarded us according to our iniquities.

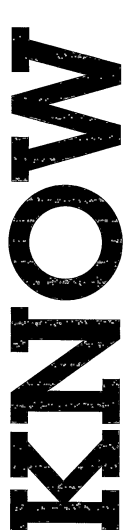

For as high as the heavens are above the earth, so great is His lovingkindness toward those who fear Him. As far as the east is from the west, so far has He removed our transgressions from us. *Psalm 103:10–12 NASB*

... I can be someone better than I was.

Therefore if anyone is in Christ, he is a new creature; the old things passed away; behold, new things have come. *2 Corinthians 5:17 NASB*

I, even I, am the one who wipes out your transgressions for My own sake, and I will not remember your sins. *Isaiah 43:25 NASB*

The thief comes only to steal and kill and destroy; I have come that they may have life, and have it to the full. *John 10:10*

... when you feel that you can't go on, he is cheering your name.

Yet those who wait for the LORD will gain new strength; they will mount up with wings like eagles, they will run and not get tired, they will walk and not become weary. *Isaiah 40:31 NASB*

He heals the brokenhearted and binds up their wounds. *Psalms 147:3*

… doing right will bring its rewards, even if not immediately.

Let us not lose heart in doing good, for in due time we will reap if we do not grow weary. *Galatians 6:9 NASB*

For the LORD God is a sun and shield; the LORD gives grace and glory; no good thing does He withhold from those who walk uprightly. *Psalm 84:11 NASB*

… when you don't feel capable, he lifts you up.

I can do all things through Him who strengthens me. *Philippians 4:13 NASB*

My flesh and my heart may fail, but God is the strength of my heart and my portion forever. *Psalm 73:26*

… he understands the struggles you face.

For we do not have a high priest who cannot sympathize with our weaknesses, but One who has been tempted in all things as we are, yet without sin. Therefore let us draw near with confidence to the throne of grace, so that we may receive mercy and find grace to help in time of need. *Hebrews 4:15–16 NASB*

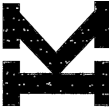

... he made the ultimate sacrifice for you.

This is how God showed his love among us: He sent his one and only Son into the world that we might live through him. This is love: not that we loved God, but that he loved us and sent his Son as an atoning sacrifice for our sins. *1 John 4:9–10*

... you can trust what he has said.

Faithful is He who calls you, and He also will bring it to pass. *1 Thessalonians 5:24 NASB*

Now behold, today I am going the way of all the earth and you know in all your hearts and in all your souls that not one word of all the good words which the LORD your God spoke concerning you has failed; all have been fulfilled for you, not one of them has failed. *Joshua 23:14 NASB*

... God has dreams so big for you that you wouldn't believe them.

Just as it is written, "things which eye has not seen and ear has not heard, and which have not entered the heart of man, all that God has prepared for those who love Him." *1 Corinthians 2:9 NASB*

"Call to me and I will answer you and tell you great and unsearchable things you do not know." *Jeremiah 33:3*

... you don't need to fear people or situations.

The LORD is my light and my salvation—whom shall I fear? The LORD is the stronghold of my life—of whom shall I be afraid? *Psalm 27:1*

God is our refuge and strength, an ever-present help in trouble. Therefore we will not fear, though the earth give way and the mountains fall into the heart of the sea, though its waters roar and foam and the mountains quake with their surging. *Psalm 46:1–3*

... you can have a sense of peace, regardless of the circumstances.

I will lie down and sleep in peace, for you alone, O LORD, make me dwell in safety. *Psalm 4:8*

LORD, you establish peace for us; all that we have accomplished you have done for us. *Isaiah 26:12*

What are you sure of?
What do you know?
What do you want?
What do you need?
Whom can you trust?
What does the best version of you believe?
When will you take the next step?

Whether you're an outcast or a crook, whether you're broken or neglected . . . here's one thing you can count on: *Jesus loves you*. Let that truth sink into you for a moment. No strings attached. He's not looking for another dollar in the offering plate, another good deed to be done. No, he simply loves you just as you are. If you give your life to him, he may very well begin to change you, but he does love you just as you are. If not, or if you have trouble believing it, remember the doubting man's response: "I believe, help my unbelief."[4]

We don't even have to fully believe that Jesus loves us for him to be real in our lives. All we have to do is give him whatever faith we have, just like the disciples gave him some bread and a few fish on that mountainside all those years ago.[5] Jesus took what they gave him, and he gave back to them. Then he did it again. And again. And again. And he fed them all. Twelve doggie bags later, the people smiled and joked with each other, completely satisfied. I imagine a happy belch or two.

That's all we have to do. Give him what we have. He'll take care of the rest.

Do you believe this?

Until then, remember this:

"Jesus loves you . . . this I know."

---

1. Dan Kimball, *They Like Jesus But Not the Church: Responding to Culture's Objections to Christianity* (Grand Rapids: Zondervan, 2008).
2. See Hebrews 11.
3. See John 14:6.
4. See Mark 9:24.
5. See Matthew 14:14–21.

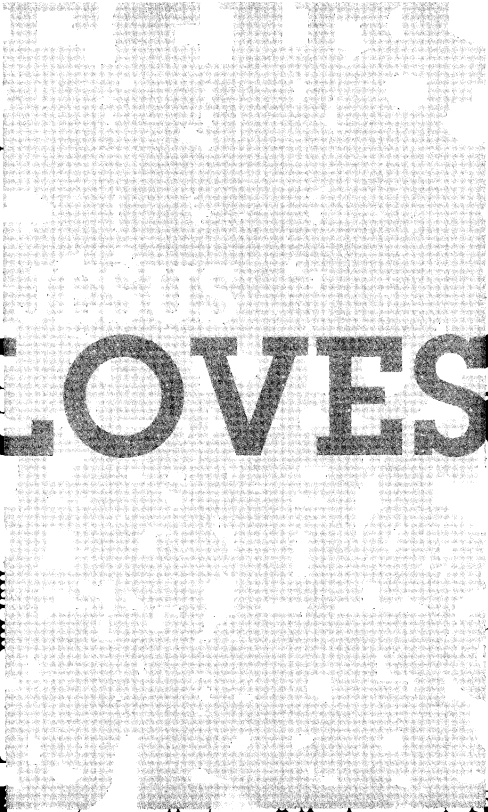

Craig Gross

Craig Gross founded Fireproof Ministries and XXXchurch. com and is the author of several books, including *The Dirty Little Secret: Uncovering the Truth Behind Porn*; *Questions You Can't Ask Your Mama about Sex*; and *Starving Jesus*. Craig recently started The Strip Church in Las Vegas. He currently lives there with his wife, Jeanette, and two kids, Nolan and Elise.

www.XXXchurch.com
www.stripchurch.com
www.craiggross.com

Jason Harper
Jason Harper founded The Extra Mile, an organization committed to advocating for better education and health care for inner-city children. Jason is the director of community outreach for Capital Christian Center. He currently lives near Sacramento with his wife, Lynette, and two kids, Madison and Josiah.
www.extramilerun.com
www.ccconline.cc
www.jasonharper.cc

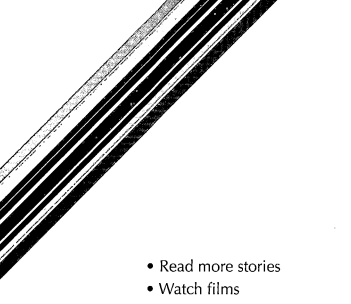

- Read more stories
- Watch films
- Share your story
- Small group curriculum
- 4-week sermon series
- Video and audio downloads
- Graphics and banners
- And much more!

Visit
www.jesuslovesyou.net

DVD Available

9780801030635 • $12.99

Individuals, small groups, congregations, and church classes will find the companion DVD an indispensable resource for learning about the world-changing love of Jesus through captivating stories and interviews. In these five films, four to six minutes each, viewers will meet face-to-face with some of the folks they encounter in the book *Jesus Loves You . . . This I Know*. Questions for groups that wish to use the films as discussion starters are available online. Also ideal for use in sermons.